ALL STALIN'S MEN

Roy Medvedev

Translated by Harold Shukman

ANCHOR PRESS/DOUBLEDAY
GARDEN CITY, NEW YORK
1984

Library of Congress Cataloging in Publication Data

Medvedev, Roy Aleksandrovich, 1925–
All Stalin's men.

Includes bibliographical references and indexes.
1. Statesmen—Soviet Union—Biography.   2. Stalin,
Joseph, 1879–1953—Friends and associates.   3. Soviet
Union—History—1917–   .   I. Title.
DK268.A1M43   1984   947.084'2'0924   83-15843
ISBN 0-385-18388-7

ANCHOR PRESS EDITION: 1984
COPYRIGHT © 1983 BY ROY MEDVEDEV
ENGLISH TRANSLATION COPYRIGHT © 1983 BY BASIL BLACKWELL PUBLISHER

Contents

Preface

This book presents six short biographies, political portraits of men who at different times were in Stalin's immediate entourage: K. Ye. Voroshilov, A. I. Mikoyan, M. A. Suslov, V. M. Molotov, L. M. Kaganovich and G. M. Malenkov. Why these six particularly out of all the people I could have chosen who were close to Stalin and wielded great power? Why not, say, G. K. Ordzhonikidze, S. M. Kirov, M. I. Kalinin and A. S. Yenukidze, who, with all their inadequacies, were the best of Stalin's entourage at the end of the 1920s and during the first half of the 1930s? Or N. I. Yezhov, L. P. Beria, G. G. Yagoda, A. N. Poskrebyshev, L. Z. Mekhlis and A. Ya. Vyshinsky, who were the worst?

The answer is simple. All these others perished or died while Stalin was still alive or did not outlive him by very long, whereas what I wanted to do was to trace the political and personal lives of men who joined the Party and began their political careers while Lenin was still alive, pursued them with comparative success under Stalin, surviving the appalling Stalinist era, and were still politically active in Khrushchev's time. These six also lived on for quite a few years into the Brezhnev era, and as I write three of them are still alive today.

All of these people played an important part in the history of the USSR and of the Communist Party of the Soviet Union. Two of them headed the Soviet government at various times; three held second place in the Party hierarchy. For decades all of them were members of the Politburo and the Council of Ministers, and their decisions affected the lives of millions of people, directly or indirectly. At the same time, their personal lives were reflections of history, mirrors held up to the different phases through which our country was living. It was on these people that Stalin – 'the Boss' in Party circles – relied; they were essential to him in the establishment of his totalitarian dictatorship. But he was essential to them too if they were to preserve their share of influence and power, and this is what makes them typical representatives of the Stalinist system.

Moreover, they were a very unfriendly lot and they all fought with each other, which was exactly what Stalin wanted. He exploited the in-fighting and mutual rivalry of the other members of the Politburo, partly on the principle of divide and rule and partly because this limited degree of 'pluralism' helped him to clarify his own ideas before presenting his proposals. He did not value friendship; he preferred certain other qualities that those around him possessed. Nearly all the people we are going to look at were diligent and energetic workers themselves, and they knew how to make their inferiors work, usually by means of intimidation and coercion. In relation to Stalin they learned only to acquiesce and to be prepared to carry out their leader's every order, even if it was criminal. Anyone who was unable to commit a criminal act was not merely removed from power but physically eliminated. This special process of selection was one through which all six of these men passed more successfully than others. They all travelled the road along which revolutionary tenacity degenerates into callousness, even sadism, political flexibility into pragmatism and enthusiasm into demagoguery. Perhaps Mikoyan alone – among the best-known – was capable of rejecting the process and forging a more humane image for himself. The rest were all perverted by the circumstances of the time in which they lived, corrupted both by the enormous power that they themselves wielded and could not refuse and by the unlimited and uncompromising authority of the leader to whom they were subject and who could destroy each of them at any moment. Not one of the people portrayed here was born a criminal or a scoundrel; it was ambition, vanity and fear that led them from one crime to the next. The circumstances in which they were placed by the Stalinist regime does not diminish their personal responsibility, however. Passing the selection test into Soviet government under Stalin depended on more than just Stalin's whim. These people worked hard to excel in his eyes and to deliver the goods that he demanded. Theirs was no ordinary competitive sport: it entailed stepping over the bodies not only of real enemies of the Party and revolution but also of people whom they themselves falsely represented as enemies of the Party and revolution.

In certain ways the people around Stalin were very much alike: fear and opportunism motivated them all. In other ways they were quite different. Some were capable of carrying out the harshest and most unjust order, knowing it to be severe and deriving no satisfaction from its execution. Others were gradually drawn into criminality and became sadists who enjoyed the orgy of savagery. Some performed their duties with the passivity of robots or professional executioners, without emotion or special commitment. Then there were those who became fanatical and dogmatic, believing that everything they did was for the good of the Party or the revolution or even 'future happiness'. They were not capable of repenting or regretting what they had done. Others were simply weak, stupid people who gave little thought to what they were doing, had no notion of what was going on around them and appeased their consciences by assuring themselves that the leadership knew best. No doubt one could identify and catalogue further types of behaviour manifested by the people with whom Stalin surrounded himself. Be that as it may. One thing is certain: the people on whom I focus in this book can be no source of pride for the USSR, the Communist Party or mankind as a whole.

To attempt biographies of even the best-known political figures in the USSR is no easy matter, for the most important aspects of their activity are shrouded in the deepest secrecy. These six men allowed people to know only what they wanted them to know. They sought publicity and fame – each one of them encouraged his own minor cult of personality – but they certainly did not permit the public to know the real facts of their political or personal lives. They made policy behind closed doors; they relaxed in government villas surrounded by high walls; and they did their best to ensure that as little document-ary material as possible would remain when they died, thus making it all the harder for the historian to reconstruct the past. I therefore beg the reader's indulgence for any possible inaccuracies, and I would be grateful for any comments and corrections. I am particularly grateful to all those who have helped me since the earliest stages of the work, for which I have been gathering material over many years.

Moscow, November 1982

1

K. Ye. Voroshilov: Red Marshal

Kliment Yefremovich Voroshilov was far less of a political personality than many of the other figures in Stalin's entourage, yet his legend greatly surpasses any of theirs. He had neither the brains nor the cunning and competence of Mikoyan, nor the organizing ability, dynamism and ruthlessness of Kaganovich, nor yet Molotov's capacity for hard work in the office. Unlike Malenkov, Voroshilov had no idea how to find his way through the labyrinth of intrigue in the Party apparatus, and he lacked both Khrushchev's enormous energy and A. A. Zhdanov's or N. A. Voznesensky's theoretical knowledge and pretensions. Even as a military leader he saw more defeats than victories. Yet perhaps it was precisely because he lacked any outstanding abilities that he managed to hold on to his place in the upper reaches of the Party and state longer than others. Indeed, as time passed the fewer his real achievements as a leader, the more colourful the legends that circulated about him. Back in 1926 the Pioneers were singing of Voroshilov, 'the first Red officer', who would make it easier for them to shed their blood. And pre-war songs included lines like, 'When Comrade Stalin sends us to fight, and the first marshal leads us into battle . . .', 'Red Marshal Voroshilov, gaze on the noble Cossack ranks . . .'. Numerous biographies of him were appearing at a time when Stalin could say – with false modesty – 'The moment hasn't yet come for a biography of Stalin.'

One thing Voroshilov did have was exceptional courage. As a soldier he often found himself in testing situations, but he would acknowledge the modesty of his intellectual ability and search for a political patron and guide. It was very important for Stalin to have just such a man at the head of the army administration, and it was also easier for a man with few outstanding features to protect his position among all of Stalin's successors.

Kliment Yefremovich Voroshilov was born on 4 February 1881. His father, Yefrem, was a retired army railway trackman, and his mother, Maria, worked as a cook and washerwoman. The family was poor and totally illiterate. Little Klim was quite uneducated too, for at the tender age of 8 he was working as a herdsboy, and at 10 he became a hand at the Golubov mine not far from Lugansk, one of the industrial centres of the Donets Basin. His mother soon took him away from the heavy work in the mine, and he was able to attend the local primary school for two sessions. When he was 15 he began working at a metal-works in Alchevsk, first as a messenger boy, then in turn as an engineer's mate on the water-tower, a metalworker in the electrical engineering shop and a crane operator in the iron foundry. It was in Alchevsk, at the age of 17, that he joined a Social Democratic circle and first read the *Communist Manifesto,* took part in his first strike, was arrested and sacked from his job and then set off on a journey (which was to last for the next three years) around the southern provinces of Russia, making ends meet with casual jobs.

He returned to the Donbas in 1903 and found a job in Lugansk, at the Hartmann Locomotive Works. It was in the same year that the Lugansk Social Democratic organization came into being, and Voroshilov joined its Bolshevik faction, soon becoming a member of the city committee.

The revolutionary events of 1905 rocked the working-class world of the Donbas. In Lugansk Voroshilov was head of both the Bolshevik committee and the soviet of workers' deputies, organizing strikes and demonstrations. He was arrested in the summer of 1905 but released on bail when thousands of workers staged a demonstration in protest.

In 1906 he was elected to represent Lugansk at the Fourth Congress of the Russian Social Democratic Labour Party. On his way to Stockholm he spent a few weeks in Petersburg, where he met Lenin for the first time and also got to know

Stalin, who still went under his Party names of Koba or Ivanovich. (Voroshilov's Party names were Volodya or Volodin.) He combined his participation in the congress with the collection of arms for Lugansk workers' combat groups and managed to arrange several arms shipments out of Finland. It was with his help that an underground printing press was set up in Lugansk, and a local Bolshevik newspaper, edited by him, began to appear.

In the following year he travelled to London to take part in the Fifth Congress of the Social Democratic Labour Party. It was at Party congresses that he got to know most of the leading Bolsheviks of the time, in particular M. V. Frunze and M. I. Kalinin. It was also in 1907 that Voroshilov met Yekaterina Davidovna Gorbman, who soon became his wife.

The revolution of 1905–07 ended in defeat; the Lugansk Bolshevik organization was destroyed; Voroshilov was arrested and exiled to the province of Archangel. From there he escaped to Baku in the Caucasus, where in 1908 he worked with Stalin in the Baku Bolshevik committee. He was soon arrested again, however, and languished until 1912 in various prisons and remote settlements in Archangel province. Released from this second exile, he returned once again to the Donbas and took up where he left off among the workers. Yet again he was arrested and this time exiled to the province of Perm, only to be released a year later under the terms of the general amnesty of 1913 on the occasion of the tercentenary of the Romanov dynasty.

It was dangerous for him to work in the Donbas, so he took a job at an iron foundry in Tsaritsyn. He was there when the First World War broke out.

Many of his fellow Bolsheviks made no attempt to evade conscription into the Army but went to the front with the aim of organizing Bolshevik agitation and preparing the Army for its part in the revolution. Voroshilov, however, did decide to evade mobilization, and to this end he took his family with him to Petrograd (as Petersburg was renamed in 1914), found work at a small boiler-making factory and made himself known to the illegal Bolshevik city committee. He was in Petrograd when the February Revolution came.

During the decisive days of February Voroshilov was in the

thick of workers' demonstrations. Earlier in the year he had made contact with some troops of the Izmailovsky Regiment and now he widened his contacts in the garrison. He was elected to represent the Izmailovsky Regiment when the Petrograd Soviet was first formed. However, he was needed back in Lugansk, and so with the Party's permission he returned to the Donbas, where he was made chairman of the town Party committee.

Thanks to the February Revolution, all political parties and groups in Russia could declare themselves openly. In Lugansk alone, counting the various nationalist organizations as well, there were fifteen different parties. The Bolsheviks quickly emerged as the most powerful of them all, numbering more than 2,500 members by the end of July. Voroshilov also represented Lugansk at the Sixth Party Congress in August 1917, which voted to prepare for eventual armed uprising. In Lugansk, however, matters were resolved without recourse to violence. By August the Bolsheviks had won a majority in the elections to the city *duma* (council); Voroshilov was elected its chairman. Then in the elections to the soviets that were held in September the Bolsheviks gained two-thirds of all the mandates, and in addition to his job as mayor Voroshilov also became chairman of the soviet. Thus both in fact and formally the Bolshevik organization of Lugansk had taken power into its own hands. Voroshilov had too much to do in the city to take time off to attend the Second All-Russian Congress of Soviets, and two other Bolsheviks went in his stead. But it was he whom the Congress elected to be a member of the All-Russian Central Executive Committee.

He returned to Petrograd in December 1917 as a deputy to the Constituent Assembly. There he took part in the work of the Third Congress of Soviets and was re-elected to the Central Executive Committee. At the request of F. E. Dzerzhinsky, first chairman of the Cheka (the secret police force, forerunner of the KGB), he was included among the first appointees to that force. His stay in the capital was prolonged by the numerous jobs he was given to do by the Central Committee and the Council of People's Commissars. For instance, we read in one directive of the Council of People's Commissars:

Comrade Voroshilov is assigned the task of liquidating the former Petrograd city governor's office in accordance with Comrade Dzerzhinsky's plan, and also the job of organizing a special force for the maintenance of peace and order in Petrograd. A commission of three people should be organized to help him with this. . . . Comrade Voroshilov is entrusted with the formation of this commission.

In February 1918, after the breakdown of peace talks and the end of the Soviet–German armistice, German troops began their advance eastwards, halted only by the signing of the Brest Litovsk peace treaty between Germany and the Russian Soviet Federal Socialist Republic (RSFSR). In the Ukraine, however, by agreement with the so-called Central Rada – the joint organ of the bourgeois parties that had seized power in Kiev and had proclaimed a Ukrainian People's Republic – the Germans continued their advance, and on 1 March they took Kiev. Countless Soviet units fell back under German pressure; workers formed detachments; and armoured trains were equipped throughout the towns of the Donbas. Under Voroshilov's leadership, a socialist partisan unit was created in Lugansk and took part in fighting around Kharkov. In the course of battle separate detachments hastily combined to form armies, one of the most powerful of which was the Fifth Ukrainian Army under the command of Voroshilov.

A Donets–Krivoy Rog Republic was declared that was based on the industrial regions of the Ukraine, but the Germans did not recognize it, and the poorly equipped Soviet armies suffered further defeat and withdrew. Voroshilov ordered his army to abandon Lugansk and to retreat to the RSFSR, but Soviet power had been overthrown in the Don province, through which his army had to move; as General Krasnov's Cossack Government had also come to terms with the Germans, the Fifth Army, and the Third Army that had joined forces with it, were placed in a very difficult position. In their first battle, at Likhaya Station, they were defeated and forced to retreat towards Belaya Kalitva. The decision was taken, however, not to disband their columns and not to abandon the refugees who were with them, but to continue moving along the railway to Tsaritsyn. Voroshilov later recalled this episode:

Tens of thousands of demoralized, exhausted, ragged people and thousands of carts carrying workers' families with all their goods and chattels had to pass through territory where the Don Cossacks raged. Surrounded on all sides by Generals Mamontov, Fitzkhalaurov, Denikin and others for three whole months, my units fought their way, restoring the railway track, which had been torn up and burned for miles on end, rebuilding bridges and shoring up embankments and dykes. After three months, the 'Voroshilov military group' reached Tsaritsyn. . . .[1]

Voroshilov's part in the defence of Tsaritsyn is without doubt a seminal episode in his military biography. To Tsaritsyn he brought 15,000 fighters, who were formed into a front division and added to several other divisions and brigades that were organized there. On orders from the Revolutionary Military Soviet, they were all combined into the Tenth Army, with Voroshilov as commander and E. A. Shchadenko as political commissar. The army included a cavalry division under B. M. Dumenko, one of whose brigades was commanded by S. M. Budyonny. Stalin, who had been in Tsaritsyn since June 1918, invested with special powers as head of provisioning in the south, assumed general responsibility for the city's defence. For several months heavy fighting took place, chiefly against General Krasnov's Cossack regiments, and with variable success. Voroshilov proved himself a brave commander; even the Cossack journal *Donetskaya Volna* (*Don Wave*) wrote of him: 'To give Voroshilov his due, even if he is not a strategist in the usual meaning of the word, there is no denying his ability to put up stubborn resistance.'[2]

The White forces were unable to take Tsaritsyn in 1918, which greatly relieved the general military position of the Soviet Republic. The Red Army was just coming into being, and Voroshilov had frequent and sharp clashes with L. D. Trotsky, who was chairman of the Revolutionary Military Soviet. The Tenth Army's actions still smacked strongly of partisan warfare; moreover, Voroshilov refused for a long time to employ former tsarist officers as military experts. Of course, he was supported in this by Stalin, to whom he was already offering almost totally unquestioning obedience. When Stalin left Tsaritsyn, Trotsky removed Voroshilov from the command of the Tenth Army. The Ukraine was by then freed from German occupation, and Voroshilov was given the job of People's Commissar for Internal Affairs of the Ukrainian Soviet Republic.

He emerged as one of the leaders of the so-called 'army opposition' at the Eighth Party Congress in 1919, where they were condemned by the majority of the delegates. Speaking of events at Tsaritsyn, Lenin said:

> The old partisan spirit is still alive in us. One can hear it in the speeches of Voroshilov and Goloshchekin. When Voroshilov speaks of the great service of the Tsaritsyn army in the defence of the city, Comrade Voroshilov is, of course, absolutely right, and such heroism would be hard to find in history. . . . But in telling his story just now, he mentioned facts that prove that there were terrible traces of partisan-mindedness. This is indisputable. Comrade Voroshilov says, 'We had no military experts, and we lost 60,000 men.' That is terrible. . . . The masses will acknowledge the heroism of the Tsaritsyn army. But to say that we did without any military experts – surely that is not defending the Party line? Comrade Voroshilov is guilty of not wanting to relinquish this old partisan state of mind. . . . Maybe we wouldn't have lost 60,000 if there had been military experts on the spot, if there had been a regular army.[3]

The civil war in the Ukraine was bitterly fought and highly complex, and Voroshilov was not left in peace to work quietly in the Ukrainian Soviet government. He took part in battles against the rebel Ataman Grigoriev, a former Red commander, and Nestor Makhno, the Anarchist leader and Ukrainian nationalist; later, in command of the Fourteenth Army, he defended Yekaterinoslav, then Kiev as a member of the Revolutionary Military Soviet with the Twelfth Army. Under pressure from General Denikin's forces, the Red Army had to abandon a great part of the Ukraine. For a time Voroshilov commanded the Sixty-First Rifle and the Seventh Cavalry divisions, and then, when the First Cavalry Army was formed, he was appointed a member of its Revolutionary Military Council. With Budyonny and Shchadenko, in the autumn of 1919, he led the First Cavalry in bitter fighting against White cavalry in central Russia and in hot pursuit of Denikin's forces. The First Cavalry played an important part in the Northern Caucasus and on the Polish front in the second half of 1920. Its final battles were against N. I. Makhno and S. V. Petlyura and, in the Tauride and the Crimea, against P. N. Wrangel.

Voroshilov was sent as the First Army's delegate to the Tenth Party Congress in 1921, where he was elected to the Congress platform and chaired several sessions. With other delegates he led a southern unit of troops to suppress the armed uprising at the Kronshtadt island garrison, just off Petrograd, where Baltic Fleet sailors were rebelling against Bolshevik authoritarianism and in favour of fully socialist soviets. For this he was decorated for the second time with the Order of the Red Banner. He appeared at the Congress with both medals pinned to his chest – which earned him some sarcastic remarks from Lenin. It was considered bad taste for Party members to parade their decorations at business meetings or even at congresses. Voroshilov turned up at the next session wearing an embroidered Ukrainian shirt and no medals. The Tenth Congress elected him to full membership of the Central Committee, which in 1921 consisted in all of only twenty-five full and fifteen candidate members.

At the end of the civil war Voroshilov continued to be involved in army work, despite the fact that he was not a professional soldier. From 1921–24 he commanded the powerful Northern Caucasus military district, where the Party leader at that time was Mikoyan, with whom Voroshilov established friendly relations. In 1923, together with Stalin and G. K. Ordzhonikidze, he became a member of the Revolutionary Military Council of the Republic and was soon a member of its presidium. The purpose of these appointments was plain – namely, to reduce the influence of Trotsky and his supporters. In May 1924 Voroshilov became commander of the Moscow military district in place of N. I. Muralov, a hero of the civil war who had distinguished himself on the Eastern Front against A. V. Kolchak. Muralov was a personal friend of Trotsky, and Stalin wanted him out of the Moscow garrison. He was sent to the Northern Caucasus military district as Voroshilov's replacement. In January 1925 the Party Central Committee accepted Trotsky's resignation; his place as People's Commissar for Military and Naval Affairs was taken by M. V. Frunze. As commander of the Moscow military district, Voroshilov was Frunze's deputy.

After only one year in charge of the Red Army in 1925 Frunze died during a bungled surgical operation. The Soviet Union at that time had a good stock of army commanders, commissars and military experts, many of whom had commanded armies, divisions and even whole fronts during the civil war and had had a hand in the planning and execution of large-scale military operations. In terms of military experience, Voroshilov was far from being the first among equals, but some of the most outstanding civil war commanders, such as M. N. Tukhachevsky, were new boys in the Bolshevik Party and had no standing in the Party hierarchy. On the other hand, those old Bolsheviks who had served with distinction in the war, such as M. N. Lashevich, though they might be members of the Party Central Committee, did not belong to any of the opposition groups, so they had no objection to the appointment of Voroshilov to the post of People's Commissar for Military and Naval Affairs. Nor were there objections in the Politburo, although 'left opposition' circles commented critically on the appointment.

I shall not dwell on Voroshilov's long and varied career as head of the Commissariat for Military and Naval affairs (later renamed the Commissariat for Defence). Against the background of capitalist encirclement no less importance was accorded to the building of a modern Red Army and Navy than to the creation of modern industry or the advancement of culture. Voroshilov had a considerable number of jobs and responsibilities, but his main functions were representative and were connected with the political control of the Army rather than with questions of military science and strategy. In this respect he differed from such prominent military leaders as B. M. Shaposhnikov, whose book *The Army's Brains* is a study of the functions of army staffs, or Tukhachevsky, who was regarded as an expert on strategy, or K. B. Kalinovsky, who studied the role of tank formations. In fact, Voroshilov never did become a professional soldier, and on many occasions he demonstrated his lack of formal military training. On the other hand, the Defence Commissariat staff during the years 1926–36 was, on the whole, of an unusually high professional calibre for that time – perhaps the best in the world.

In 1926 Voroshilov became a member of the Politburo. It goes without saying that, unlike many military and military-political staff who took part in the 'left opposition', he would invariably side with Stalin and the Central Committee majority.

He had played an honourable part in the civil war, but many others had distinguished themselves more and had rendered more valuable service. Even in the matter of military decorations Voroshilov trailed somewhat. V. K. Blyukher, for instance, who was the first man to receive the Order of the Red Banner, had been awarded five such medals by the end of the war, while Y. F. Fabritsius and I. F. Fedko had each received four. Voroshilov (who was decorated three times in all) was a vain man, and this was a failing that Stalin could and did exploit. Nevertheless, around Voroshilov a legend began to grow up, a sort of private cult of the 'worker–commander'. Within a year of his appointment as Commissar the first biographies of him began to appear, as well as tales of his exploits.[4] The poet and writer K. N. Altaisky wrote a collection of tales and a poem about Voroshilov, as did the 90-year-old Kazakh folk poet Dzh. Dzhambul.

He was quick to repay the debt. At the end of 1929 a long article by him appeared in the Soviet press entitled 'Stalin and the Red Army', which effectively laid the foundation for the legend of Stalin as the most powerful commander of the civil war and the architect of the Red Army's chief victories. He wrote:

> In 1918–1920 Stalin was perhaps the only man whom the Central Committee sent from one battle front to another, selecting the places that were most dangerous and threatening to the revolution. Stalin was not to be found where things were quiet and were going well, where we were enjoying success; but wherever the Red Armies were cracking and the counter-revolutionary forces were threatening the very existence of Soviet power, there you would find Comrade Stalin.[5]

In 1929, of course, a certain caution still had to be exercised in falsifying history. Voroshilov inserts the word 'perhaps' and speaks of Stalin as 'one of the most outstanding architects of victories in the civil war'. In another ten years he would be able to dispense with all such reservations. In a 1939 article entitled 'Stalin and the Formation of the Red Army' he wrote:

> Many volumes will be written about Stalin, creator of the Red Army and architect of its victories, author of laws of strategy and tactics in the proletarian revolution. We, his contemporaries and comrades-in-arms, can provide only a few sketches of his vast and fruitful military work.[6]

At the end of the 1920s Voroshilov still retained some features of his own personality. In 1928–29, when Stalin unleashed his real offensive against the peasants, Voroshilov frequently expressed doubts at Politburo sessions about the rightness of the policy. He feared that the peasants' discontent would be reflected in the fighting power of the Red Army, which was drawn in the main from peasant youth. Rumours of these objections became so exaggerated that in some of his letters Trotsky, who was already in exile abroad, referred to the possibility of a peasant uprising against Stalin, under the leadership of Voroshilov and Budyonny. And when the writer Isaac Babel published his famous cycle of stories *Red Cavalry* in 1926, he was accused of slander by an enraged Budyonny – even critics of the time were hostile to the tales – yet Voroshilov came to his defence, in the company of Maxim Gorky. During the 1930s, however, Voroshilov progressively shed his independence and was drawn more and more under Stalin's influence and power.

In the early 1930s he was at the centre of Stalin's entourage and was regarded as his intimate friend. They would sit together on the platform at meetings, stand side by side on the Mausoleum, go hunting together, take holidays in the south, spend time at Stalin's dacha and at his apartment in the Kremlin. They often visited Maxim Gorky after he had returned to the USSR for good. In the Gorky Museum in Moscow one can still see Gorky's book containing the poem

'Death and the Maiden' and bearing Stalin's inscription: 'This piece is stronger than Goethe's *Faust:* love conquers death.' On the opposite page Voroshilov's response opens with these words: 'I'm not a literate man. . . .'

Voroshilov travelled abroad on several occasions. He discovered that one was expected to dance at receptions but was at a loss, as he knew none of the steps. An army officer who did not know how to dance seemed to provoke an odd reaction in the West, so on his initiative, in nearly all the large cities in the USSR and in officers' clubs in garrison towns, officers began to be instructed in the latest European dances, which had been so scorned by the Komsomol of the 1920s.

Far more important, to be sure, than introducing dancing into army life was the intensive technical rearming of the Red Army that was instigated at the beginning of the 1930s, at the same time as the forced industrialization of the country. The Party made it plain that the development of an arms industry and the technical equipping of the Army and the Navy were to be among the primary aims of the first and second Five-Year Plans. Until 1930 the Red Army had still been equipped mainly with arms supplied during the First World War and the civil war. From 1930 to 1934, however, it took delivery of a large number of new tanks, quantities of artillery and communications and chemical equipment. A special effort was made to enlarge the Air Force with bombers and other types of aircraft, and the Navy was also expanded and modernized. Speaking at the Seventeenth Party Congress in February 1934, Voroshilov asserted that the Red Army was now better equipped technically than either the French or the American armies and that it was more mechanized than even the British Army, which was regarded at that time as the best in the world from the technical point of view.

After the Seventeenth Congress the Voroshilov cult burgeoned. It was the custom in those days to give the names of the leaders to towns and villages, so Lugansk was duly renamed Voroshilovgrad, several other towns, factories, collective farms and mountain peaks acquired his name, and a heavy tank was called the KV in his honour. Yet as the management of the Red Army became more complicated, so Voroshilov's incapacity to resolve the difficult problems raised by army organization became manifest. Differences arose in the Revolutionary Military Council because Voroshilov and Budyonny continued to exaggerate the role of heavy cavalry formations during a future war. Changes were clearly essential.

The People's Commissariat for Defence was reorganized in 1934. M. N. Tukhachevsky was appointed one of Voroshilov's deputies. In her book on Tukhachevsky Lidia Nord quotes Tukhachevsky's opinion of Voroshilov:

> 'Everything will be different,' continued Tukhachevsky. 'For three weeks, day and night, since entering the Defence Council, Voroshilov, Yegorov, Blyukher, Ordzhonikidze and I have been poring over plans. It has to be said that Voroshilov is not very clever, but he has at least the virtue that he does not try to be clever, and he agrees eagerly with everything. . . .'[7]

Lidia Nord knew Tukhachevsky personally for many years, and while her book is in some respects reliable, it also repeats rumour and gossip, which greatly diminishes its value as a source. However, Tukhachevsky's opinion of Voroshilov could hardly have been different. He had valued Frunze very highly and did not regard Voroshilov as an authority on purely military affairs (if, indeed, he looked on him as a professional soldier at all). He was not alone in forming a rather low opinion of Voroshilov's intellectual capacity.

The terror of 1936–38 fell with special ferocity on the military cadres. It is no exaggeration to claim that during those years the main structure of the Soviet Army and Navy, consisting of its best elements, was pitilessly destroyed. The victims died not on the battlefield but in the cellars of the Lubyanka and other prisons and concentration camps. No one knows the precise figure, but one may estimate with a reasonable degree of certainty that between 25,000 and 30,000 regular officers and military-political staff in the Army and Navy perished.

The rank of marshal had been introduced in 1935 and bestowed on five commanders – Voroshilov, Budyonny, V. K. Blyukher, Tukhachevsky and A. I. Yegorov. Three years later

Blyukher, Tukhachevsky and Yegorov were shot as 'enemies of the people'. According to the incomplete figures, out of 16 army commanders, first- and second-class, 15 perished; out of 67 corps commanders, 60; out of 199 divisional commanders, 136; out of 397 brigade commanders, 221. All 4 Admirals of the Fleet (Naval Flag Officers) died; all 6 full admirals; 9 of the 15 vice-admirals; all 17 army commissars, first- and second-class; 25 of the 29 corps commissars. Of 97 divisional commissars and 36 brigade commissars 79 and 34 respectively were arrested; and one-third of all regimental commanders were condemned.

What was the role of People's Commissar Voroshilov in this fearful massacre of the military cadres? We have no proof that it was actually Voroshilov who compiled the blacklists of those to be arrested and shot, but Stalin did not need Voroshilov for that. It was enough that Voroshilov should sanction all the arrests and that he should sign most of the lists, together with Stalin and Yezhov. None of the high-ranking army men could have been arrested without the knowledge and concurrence of the People's Commissar for Defence – and Voroshilov always gave his consent. He also helped to kindle the spy mania that swept through the Army and Navy. In August 1937 – that is, immediately after the court-martial and execution of Tukhachevsky, I. E. Yakir, I. P. Uborevich, B. M. Feldman, A. I. Kork and others, and after Voroshilov's deputy, Ya. B. Gamarnik, had committed suicide – Defence Commissar Voroshilov and Internal Affairs Commissar Yezhov signed a joint decree for the Armed Forces of the USSR in which it was stated that a network of spies from various countries had spread throughout the Soviet Union, especially in the Red Army; anyone who had the slightest contact with spies was ordered to confess and anyone with any knowledge or suspicion about espionage activities was instructed to report them.

In several cases Voroshilov collaborated directly with the organs of repression. When NKVD agents appeared in the office of I. F. Fedko, Voroshilov's first deputy since the executions of Tukhachevsky and Gamarnik, Fedko put up armed resistance and ordered his guards to hold the men at gunpoint while he telephoned his boss. Voroshilov said that he would look into the matter at once and ordered Fedko to yield to the

NKVD 'temporarily', Fedko was shot soon after, on an order that had been signed no doubt by Voroshilov as well as by Stalin and Yezhov. A number of Soviet military attachés were recalled to Moscow for an audience with Voroshilov, only to be arrested in the Defence Commissar's reception room. This kind of thing could have occurred only with his agreement and approval.

When Hitler was preparing to attack the USSR, he could refer, without beating about the bush, to the destruction of the Soviet military cadres as a factor in Germany's favour. 'The very best staff among the highest Soviet military cadres have been destroyed by Stalin,' he told Keitel. 'This means that the generation that is coming up to replace them still lacks the necessary minds.'

The debilitating effects of the mass repressions against the Army were to be felt during the course of the Soviet–Finnish War of 1939–40. Stalin had reckoned that this would be a short and relatively inexpensive military operation, but the weeks turned into months and still the Soviet forces were unable to break through the Finnish line of defence, despite the dozens of divisions that were committed to the fight against Finland. Voroshilov was personally in charge of military operations and made frequent visits to the front; but every kilometre taken from the enemy was strewn, literally, with the bodies of Soviet soldiers. Stalin was greatly angered by the Red Army's tremendous losses and its minimal successes. In the end, it is true, the Soviet union got the upper hand, but the victory was purchased at a terrible price.

The results of the Finnish campaign were analysed in April 1940 at an enlarged session of the Chief Military Council, at which L. Z. Mekhlis, head of the Military Political Directorate, spoke bluntly and at length about the blunders committed by Defence Commissar Voroshilov. Some speakers took issue with Mekhlis, but it was plain that argument itself was feasible only because it had been sanctioned by Stalin. In the end it was agreed that the Red Army's fighting capacity should be increased; Stalin secretly issued the order to rehabilitate and release a number of incarcerated army officers; and the decision

was taken to relieve Voroshilov of his post and to replace him
with S. K. Timoshenko. Timoshenko had commanded a regiment at the defence of Tsaritsyn and had been a divisional
commander in the First Cavalry. After Yakir's execution he had
run the Kiev military district and since January 1940 had
commanded troops on the Finnish front.

The blow to Voroshilov's prestige was softened somewhat
by the fact that he was awarded the Order of Lenin and given
the job of deputy chairman of the Council of People's Commissars. His real influence in the Party and military hierarchy,
however, had clearly diminished.

The Second World War began with heavy losses for the Red
Army. Even by the end of the first day Hitler's troops had
achieved tangible successes, while the People's Commissariat
and the General Staff were beginning to lose control over the
troops. Stalin isolated himself in his dacha for several days and
would receive nobody. Timoshenko assumed command of
General Headquarters, created on 23 June 1941, while G. K.
Zhukov was given the important job of heading the General
Staff. The situation on the main western front was especially
difficult; GHQ dispatched Marshals Shaposhnikov, Kulik and
Voroshilov to the front, though they were unable to claw back
any ground or even to regain control over the troops and make
the retreat more orderly. In view of the rout and the chaotic
withdrawal of so many units, Voroshilov and Shaposhnikov
proposed the formation of a new line of defence, much further
to the east of the river Berezina, along the middle Dnieper,
although in the event the German advance was merely halted –
temporarily – still further to the east, in the battles for
Smolensk.

The responsibility for the defeats of the first phase of the war
rested primarily on Stalin, of course, but Voroshilov's share
was considerable. He was guilty of permitting the massacre of
the military cadres; he had made reassuring speeches to the
country to the effect that the Red Army had weapons more
powerful than those of any other army, whereas the truth was
that the German Army had the advantage in most kinds of
armament. As Defence Commissar, he had greatly exaggerated

the role of cavalry formations in a future war and had failed to promote the necessary sophistication of tank formations and anti-aircraft units.

On 1 July 1941 Voroshilov was recalled to Moscow. Stalin had resumed the leadership of the country and of the Army; the State Defence Committee had been created and Voroshilov was appointed a member. Stalin was in charge of Supreme Command HQ, Budyonny of south-western and Timoshenko of western defence. Voroshilov, in command of defence in the north-west, arrived in Leningrad with a small staff on 11 July in order to take command of the retreating forces. Young soldiers and even schoolboys started to sing a new refrain:

> The call rings out, forward to victory!
> The people have faith in their commanders.
> Lead us, Voroshilov, Timoshenko and Budyonny,
> Lead us in the sacred campaign!

This verse had apparently been added to an old song after the decision was taken to set up the three sectors of defence; but barely a month was to pass before the song was proscribed and people were beginning to have doubts about their military leaders.

The battered and exhausted troops were not particularly heartened by the arrival in Leningrad of Voroshilov and his staff – their commanders remembered the unsuccessful Finnish campaign. The Red Army's retreat in the Baltic region continued, and only on isolated sectors of the front did its engagements meet with intermittent success. Moreover, the Finnish army, weakened by the recent war, was not especially active in those weeks. The front line gradually moved to the east, and the numbers of Soviet troops and their weapons diminished. The position was made more complicated by the need to evacuate from the Baltic, mainly through Leningrad, hundreds of thousands of people and a multitude of enterprises.

It proved in the end impossible to halt the Germans in the north-west, and by August the Nazi troops had already reached the distant approaches to Leningrad. Voroshilov acted bravely but incompetently. He had plenty of nerve and often drove out to the front line of the defence, squarely in the enemy's view. What he lacked was firmness in his command of the troops. At the end of August Leningrad was virtually surrounded and deprived of a railway link with the rest of the country. On 1 September Voroshilov received the following cable from Stalin:

> GHQ regards tactics of Leningrad front ruinous. Leningrad front thinks only of one thing – how to withdraw, only to find new lines of withdrawal. Is it not time to have done with heroes of retreat? GHQ authorizes your retreat for the last time and demands Leningrad front take courage honourably and staunchly uphold the cause for the defence of Leningrad.

Nevertheless, the retreat went on; with the fall of Shlissel-burg, by 9–10 September Leningrad was surrounded. On 10 September Voroshilov personally led a marine attack, but it was if anything an act of desperation, and on the same day he was removed from his post. Command of the front was handed over to Zhukov, who at once brusquely rejected Voroshilov's offers of advice. Under Zhukov's command the storming of Leningrad, which began in September, was rebuffed. As GHQ's representative, Voroshilov spent some time helping his friend G. I. Kulik, commander of the Fifty-Fourth Army, who was trying to break through from the east in an effort to assist Leningrad. But Marshal Kulik turned out to be incapable of leading an army astutely, and he suffered defeat. He too was removed from his post and severely punished, whereas Stalin had mercy on Voroshilov and ordered the State Defence Committee to post him to a job checking the training of Red Army reserves in the Moscow, Volga, Central Asian and Urals military districts.

In September 1942 he was appointed commander-in-chief of the partisan movement, with authority over its central headquarters, then under the leadership of P. K. Ponomarenko, first secretary of the Belorussian Party Central Committee. In fact, Ponomarenko remained in charge of the partisan movement, as Voroshilov's participation was erratic and merely formal in nature. As the Red Army began its westward advance, Voroshilov was made chairman of the committee responsible for captured enemy property; in addition, he carried out several diplomatic missions – he held talks with the British military mission, for example, and chaired commissions for armistices with Finland, Hungary and Romania.

After the war Voroshilov abandoned military affairs for good and, as a member of the Politburo and the Bureau of the Council of Ministers, was instead put in charge of a number of boards dealing with cultural matters, with which he had dealt even before the war. He had, for example, engaged in a correspondence with the great Russian artist Ilya Repin, whom Stalin was very keen to persuade to return to the USSR. But that had been when he was still head of the Defence Committee of the Council of People's Commissars, whereas now he was in charge of the Cultural Bureau of the Council of Ministers. This body supervised the activities of the country's theatres, the Committee for Cinematographic Affairs and book publishing. In Voroshilov's Kremlin office one was likely now to encounter directors, managers of large publishing houses and artists rather than generals. Naturally, he was not involved in important cultural issues; thus it was Stalin's approval, not Voroshilov's, that was needed to screen a film. The director M. I. Romm once had a long discussion with Voroshilov about making a series of documentary films to mark the tenth anniversary of the battle of Moscow. He formed the impression that Voroshilov was not so much in charge of culture as 'attached' to it, and that even though he was a member of the Politburo, he was afraid to decide any question on his own authority. At the end of the conversation Voroshilov said, 'I feel I am getting older and more stupid.'

There is a story that in 1949 an attempt was made to arrest his wife who, like Molotov's, was Jewish. Voroshilov is supposed to have grabbed either a sword or a pistol and to have chased the security men out of his apartment. The whole story is a fabrication, however: there was never any attempt to arrest his wife, though some of his relations were arrested, and he himself fell into deeper disgrace at Stalin's 'court', where he was the target of contempt and distrust.

At a session of the Politburo some time after the war the

question of finding ways to modernize the Soviet Navy was
under discussion. As was his custom, Stalin asked everyone
present, which included top naval men who had been specially
invited, for their opinions, keeping the last word for himself.
Voroshilov turned out to hold a minority view; Stalin, advancing his own arguments as he wound up the discussion, sided
with the majority. But he did not merely reject Voroshilov's
points – he repeated three times the ominous statement, 'I don't
understand why Comrade Voroshilov wants to weaken the
Soviet Navy.' He then invited everyone to join him to watch
the film *Ogni bolshogo goroda* (*A Great City in Flames*), which he
had already seen dozens of times.

The deputy head of the Navy, Admiral-of-the-Fleet I. S.
Isakov, wrote down his impressions of the meeting the minute
he got home that night. Apparently, little tables were laid with
cold snacks in the small room where the film was being shown,
but nobody would sit with Voroshilov. Yet when the lights
went up at the end of the film Stalin turned around and, seeing
Voroshilov all by himself, suddenly got up, went over to him
and laid a hand on his shoulder. Turning to Beria, he said,
'Lavrenty, we really should take care of Voroshilov. It's not
as though there are many old Bolsheviks like him around.
We must look after him.' No-one said a word, as the guests
were not sure why Stalin had addressed this remark to Beria in
particular.

Stalin was not content with merely keeping Voroshilov at a
distance; he went out of his way, in the presence of other
Central Committee members, to express a lack of political
confidence in him and on occasion even declared Voroshilov to
be nothing less than a British spy! There were times when
Voroshilov was not invited to meetings of the Politburo, and
often, on hearing of an impending meeting, he would ring up
Stalin's secretary, A. M. Poskrebyshev, and humbly ask,
'Please could you find out if I can come to the Politburo
meeting?'

Despite all that, he did preside over a number of sessions at
the Nineteenth Party Congress in 1952 and even gave the brief
closing address, though Stalin made his own speech after the
Congress had formally ended. Voroshilov was appointed to the

enlarged Central Committee Presidium (Politburo) and also to its inner Bureau of nine.

Only two people in the leadership, Molotov and Voroshilov, used the familiar form of 'you' (*ty*) when addressing Stalin right up to his death, and Voroshilov often even called him by his old revolutionary nickname, Koba.

Voroshilov was involved in the discussions about the question of power-sharing that took place among Party and state leaders immediately after Stalin's death. The post of chairman of the Presidium of the Supreme Soviet was occupied at that time by N. M. Shvernik, who before the war had been head of the Soviet trade unions, but was then only a candidate member of the Politburo with little influence. It was decided that he should return to being head of the trade unions and that his job as head of state (that is, chairman of the Presidium of the Supreme Soviet) should go to Voroshilov.

Voroshilov supported Malenkov and Khrushchev in their plan to remove Beria; in fact, he not only agreed to it but burst into tears of emotion after Malenkov had discussed the matter with him. For too long he had lived with the fear that Beria would 'take care of him', as Stalin had recommended.

The friendly collaboration between Khrushchev and Voroshilov did not last long, however, and Voroshilov supported Molotov, Malenkov and Kaganovich when they came out against Khrushchev in June 1957. But he was not a reliable ally, for although he was greatly alarmed by Khrushchev's determination to expose Stalin's crimes and was firmly opposed to his intention to speak out at the Twentieth Party Congress, when Voroshilov realized that the full Central Committee was not going to support its own Presidium, he reverted to Khrushchev and made a speech resolutely condemning Molotov and his friends. (For this reason his name is not included in the plenum's resolutions on the 'anti-Party group'.) Soon afterwards, in a speech that he gave in Leningrad in early July, he once again condemned the 'vile attempt' by Molotov, Malenkov and Kaganovich to attack the 'Leninist leadership' of the Central Committee in the person of Comrade N. S. Khrushchev. As a result, he managed to retain his position as head of state for a few more years, though he was to exhibit neither a glimmer of statesmanship nor the least initiative in the job. Those who were able to observe him closely, however, were surprised by a new trait that he had acquired: avarice. It seems that he was extremely unwilling to hand over to the state the rich gifts that he was often given as head of state on his trips abroad or when receiving foreign heads of state in Moscow; he apparently did his best to keep them for himself.

His disloyalty in 1957 was not forgotten. Lugansk, which had been renamed Voroshilovgrad in 1935, was given back its old name in 1958. In 1960, with due ceremony and after the title of Hero of Socialist Labour had been bestowed on him to the accompaniment of appropriate speeches, Voroshilov, then aged 79, was relieved of his duties as chairman of the Presidium of the Supreme Soviet, although he remained one of its members. His place as chairman was taken by the 53-year-old L. I. Brezhnev.

While Molotov, Malenkov and Kaganovich were absent from the Twenty-Second Party Congress in 1961, Voroshilov was there, not merely as a delegate but as one of the leadership, a member of the Congress presidium. He therefore had to sit and listen to the accusations that were hurled at his recent comrades-in-arms and to not a few that were directed at himself. Speaking in his report to Congress about the factional 'anti-Party group', Khrushchev named Voroshilov among its most active participants and went on to say that Voroshilov's position had been no accident, for he also bore personal responsibility for 'many of the massive repressions that had been carried out against Party, soviet, economic, military and Komsomol cadres, and for other similar phenomena that occurred during the period of the cult of personality'.[8] Voroshilov was mentioned by nearly all the other speakers when they referred to the 'anti-Party group'. The chairman of the Council of Ministers, A. S. Polyansky, was especially sharp and explicit in his condemnation of Voroshilov, stating among other things:

> Everybody knows of his earlier service to the Motherland. That is why the Central Committee has been very indulgent towards

him. But you took an active part in that group, Comrade Voroshilov, even if, as you claim, you were 'led astray by the devil'. We don't think the devil had anything to do with it. You wanted to erase all traces of your part in the repression of totally innocent people – especially the cadres of the military leadership – which the whole country knows about.

As a member of the anti-Party group, and an active one at that, Comrade Voroshilov was impertinent, rude and provocative. He even refused to meet members of the Central Committee at the critical moment when they wanted to convene a plenum. He forgot that they had elected him to the Presidium of the Central Committee and that they could therefore withdraw the considerable trust that they had placed in him. And how did he conduct himself at the Central Committee plenum? I will recall just one episode. When Kaganovich was accused of committing mass terror in the Kuban, carried out on his orders and in his presence, Voroshilov sprang to his defence. Leaping to his feet and waving his fists, he shouted, 'You're still young! We'll straighten you out!' We replied: 'Calm down, the Central Committee will decide who needs straightening out.'

So, Comrade Voroshilov, don't try to come the innocent with us. You must bear your full share of responsibility for your anti-Party activities, just like the rest of the anti-Party group.[9]

Voroshilov was very agitated during Polyansky's speech. He stood up, sat down, and finally threw his writing pad on the table in anger and left the hall. But he turned up the next day and again sat through speeches in which his name was mentioned. For instance, A. N. Shelepin, who had become head of the KGB in 1958, disclosed the following information about Voroshilov:

The night before his execution Yakir wrote a letter to Voroshilov: 'To K. Ye. Voroshilov. In memory of many years of honourable work that I did for the Red Army, I ask you to make sure that my family is looked after and to give them help, as they are helpless and entirely innocent. . . .' Yet on this letter, from a man with whom he had worked for many years and who, as he knew well, had looked death in the face on more than one occasion, Voroshilov could write, 'I doubt the integrity of this dishonest man altogether.'[10]

Many of the delegates demanded the expulsion from the Party of the 'anti-Party group'. However, a statement by Voroshilov was read out at the nineteenth session of the Congress on 27 October. In it he asserted that although he had supported the 'mistaken, harmful speeches of the anti-Party group' in June 1957, he had had 'no idea of the group's factional activities'. The statement went on:

> Deeply aware of the great harm that could have been done to our Party and country by the anti-Party group of Molotov, Malenkov, Kaganovich and others, I absolutely condemn their factional activity, which was aimed at diverting the Party from its Leninist path. I fully understand the seriousness of my error in supporting the harmful speeches of the anti-Party group.[11]

Concerning his part in the Stalinist terror, Voroshilov stated:

> I am entirely in agreement with the great task that the Party has undertaken to restore Leninist norms to Party life and to eliminate the violations of revolutionary legality introduced during the period of the cult of personality, and I deeply regret that I also committed errors in that context.[12]

During his summing-up at the following session, Khrushchev condemned Voroshilov but called upon the delegates to show magnanimity:

> I have something particular to say about Comrade Voroshilov. He came to tell me about his suffering. But we are political people; we cannot be guided by emotion alone. Feelings vary. They can be deceptive. Here at the Congress Voroshilov hears criticism of his actions and goes about like a beaten man. But you should have seen him when the anti-Party group raised its hand against the Party. Then he was extremely energetic and rode out with his colours flying, like a knight in shining armour. . . . It was no accident that the factionalists chose him to meet the Central Committee members who were trying to convene a plenum. The anti-Party group was counting on his authority to influence them and to shake [the Central Committee's] resolve in its struggle against the anti-Party group. . . .

Comrade Voroshilov has made serious mistakes, but I think, comrades, that we should approach him differently from the way in which we approach the other members of the group, like Molotov, Malenkov and Kaganovich. . . . The name of Kliment Yefremovich Voroshilov is widely known among the people; therefore his membership of the anti-Party group that included Molotov, Malenkov and Kaganovich somewhat strengthened the group and made a certain impression on people who are not well versed in politics. By leaving the group Comrade Voroshilov has helped the Central Committee in its struggle against the factionalists. Let us respond to his good deed in kind; let us alleviate his distress. Comrade Voroshilov has been sharply criticized, and rightly so, for he has made serious errors, which Communists cannot forget. But I think that we should treat him with consideration and should show magnanimity. I believe that he genuinely condemns his own actions and that he repents of them.[13]

Voroshilov was 'forgiven' in that he was not expelled from the Party, but he was included neither in the new composition of the Central Committee nor in any other important Party institution. His own articles stopped appearing in the press, as did articles about him. He quitted public and political life almost completely and rarely attended meetings of the Supreme Soviet, though he was elected to it in both 1962 and 1966.

Voroshilov was not deprived of the privileges that he had previously enjoyed, and he lived out his remaining years quietly at his country estate outside Moscow. His family was small. His wife had died, and they had had no children of their own, although he did bring up Frunze's daughter and an adopted son, Peter, who gave him two grandsons, Klim and Volodya. He began to write his memoirs in the mid-1960s, which was no doubt why he started visiting the Lenin Library, where his daughter-in-law, Peter's wife, worked. Despite the denunciations of the Twenty-Second Congress, his legend was still alive in the minds of the Soviet people, and he was therefore regarded by the public somewhat differently from Molotov or Kaganovich.

On one occasion when I was working in the great researcher's reading room at the Lenin Library, applause suddenly broke out behind me. I turned, and there at the end of the hall, coming down the steps out of the newspaper room, was Voroshilov. Nearly everybody in the hall – and there were a good thousand of them – rose to give him an ovation. To the thunder of applause, he walked slowly down the aisle between the tables towards the exit. Only five or six people remained silent and in their seats. Among them I spotted Yakir's son, Peter, who could barely restrain himself from shouting abuse at Voroshilov and at the researchers who were giving him such a warm reception.

As a matter of fact, after Khrushchev's removal sympathy for Voroshilov began to be shown at an even higher level, in the context of the partial rehabilitation of Stalin that extremely influential circles attempted to bring about after the October 1964 plenum of the Central Committee. After an interval of five years, at the Twenty-Third Party Congress in 1966, Voroshilov was again elected a member of the Central Committee. The newspapers and magazines started to carry articles about him, and fragments of his memoirs appeared. A number of army people and intellectuals protested. The military historian Lieutenant-Colonel V. A. Anfilov, speaking in the spring of 1966 at a meeting in the Institute of Marxism–Leninism at which A. M. Nekrich's book *22 June 1941* was under discussion, said, 'My heart bleeds when I see him [Voroshilov] standing on Lenin's mausoleum.' But the protests led nowhere. In 1968 celebrations took place to mark the fiftieth anniversary of the formation of the Red Army. High honours were awarded to Voroshilov during the jubilee: he received his second Gold Star and a sword of honour bearing the arms of the USSR in gold. The city authorities of Rostov-on-Don bestowed on him the title of 'honoured citizen'. That year saw the publication of his first book of memoirs, called *Tales of Life,* devoted mainly to the Lugansk period of his activity. Describing his first meeting with Stalin, he felt constrained to give a general assessment of the man:

We made friends and I soon discovered that my new friend was a Georgian called Yosif Vissarionovich Dzhugashvili. . . . Thus by sheer chance I first happened to meet the man who, under the name of Stalin, would go down firmly in the history of our Party and the country. He lived a long and complicated life. Though it was darkened by serious, notorious mistakes, I cannot speak of him without respect, and I regard it as my duty, when I come to the final stage of my memoirs, to say truthfully everything I know about him that has remained indelibly in my memory.[14]

Given an introduction like that, it was hard to believe that Voroshilov really would truthfully record everything that he could remember, but he did not anyway have the chance to continue writing his memoirs. He died on 3 December 1969 and was buried with honour in a grave by the Kremlin wall. The town of Lugansk was once again renamed Voroshilovgrad, and much has been done since his death to restore his legend, though it is unlikely to outlive Voroshilov himself by very long.

2

A. I. Mikoyan: from Ilyich to Ilyich

Anastas Ivanovich Mikoyan died in October 1978, just one month short of his eighty-third birthday. His was a most instructive life, an uncommon example of political survival under Soviet conditions. As early as 1919 he was elected to the All-Russian Central Executive Committee of the Russian Soviet Federative Socialist Republic, then to the Central Executive Committee of the USSR and the Presidium of the Supreme Soviet of the USSR, of which he remained a member until 1974. This means that Mikoyan occupied posts in the highest reaches of the Soviet administration for fifty-five years, for all but one of which he was a member of the Party Central Committee (and for forty of those he was in the Politburo). With the exception of Voroshilov, there has never been anybody in the leadership of either the Party or the state with more seniority than Mikoyan. When he started to publish fragments of his memoirs in the late 1960s somebody quipped that they ought to be called 'From Ilyich [Lenin] to Ilyich [Brezhnev]'.

Such peerless political longevity indicates more than exceptional qualities of statesmanship – it points to a capacity for rapid adaptation to sudden changes in the political environment. Perhaps he was lucky – but then not everyone is smart enough to take advantage of lucky breaks. Mikoyan's gift for manoeuvring is still the subject of jokes among Party members. One goes like this. Mikoyan is visiting friends. Suddenly it starts raining heavily outside; all the same, Mikoyan gets up to go home. 'But you can't walk!' his friends protest. 'It's pouring out there, and you haven't got an umbrella!' 'Don't worry,' he says, 'I can dodge between the raindrops.'

Anastas Ivanovich Mikoyan, the son of a poor carpenter, was born in the Armenian village of Senain in 1895. He was a clever child, and after primary school his father sent him to the Nerseyan Armenian Seminary in Tiflis, which was one of the best educational establishments in the Caucasus. It was open to all classes of the population and offered a better education than the grammar schools. Few of its products ended up as priests, but many of them became prominent members of the Armenian intelligentsia. Strange as it may seem, the theological seminaries in Russia produced quite a few revolutionaries – such as N. G. Chernyshevsky and N. A. Dobrolyubov – and Stalin himself attended a seminary in Tiflis. In fact, dozens and dozens of prominent Soviet state and Party figures of the 1920s and 1930s were educated at seminaries. Mikoyan's closest friend at school was Georg Alikhanyan, who later became one of the founders of Soviet Armenia and a leading figure in Comintern, only to be shot at the end of the 1930s. His daughter, Elena, is the wife of Academician A. D. Sakharov.

It was while he was still at the seminary that Mikoyan joined a Social Democrat circle and read virtually everything of Marx that had been translated into Russian. In the same year that he joined the Bolshevik Party, 1915, he completed the seminary course with flying colours and entered the Armenian Theological Academy at Echmyadzin, the religious centre of Armenia. But instead of becoming a priest, at the time of the February Revolution he devoted himself to organizing the Echmyadzin Soviet of Soldiers' Deputies.

Soon after the October Revolution Mikoyan found himself doing Party work in Baku, the major industrial centre and Bolshevik stronghold in the Trans-Caucasus. The Baku Soviet included Bolsheviks, Mensheviks, Dashnaks (Armenian nationalists), Socialist Revolutionaries and others, but in April 1918 the Bolsheviks, with their insignificant majority, succeeded in creating a Council of People's Commissars headed by S. G. Shaumyan, a member of the Central Committee of the Bolshevik Party, whom, at Lenin's suggestion, the Soviet Government had appointed Special Commissar for Caucasian affairs as early as December 1917.

Mikoyan commanded a Bolshevik armed detachment that took part in the suppression of a Musavatist (Azerbaijan nationalist) rising that was supported by Turkish troops and was advancing on the city. Baku was not easy to defend. The civil war had begun. The Cossack rising on the Don and in the Northern Caucasus, as well as the Czech rebellion and the advance of General Denikin's Volunteer Army, all combined to cut off the Baku commune from the rest of revolutionary Russia. The Trans-Caspian region of Central Asia was occupied by the British, and the civilian administration there was in the hands of the Socialist Revolutionaries. The only means by which the Baku Communists could get help from Soviet Russia was by sea, through Astrakhan. In these circumstances the Socialist Revolutionaries and Mensheviks in the Soviet proposed that the British forces be asked to enter Baku. The First World War was still being waged; Britain and Turkey were fighting. The Bolsheviks opposed the suggestion, but they were outvoted in a stormy session. By 258 to 236 the Baku Soviet agreed to invite in the British forces and to form a coalition Government of all the parties in the Soviet. Some of the Bolsheviks proposed that their Council of People's Commissars be preserved and that there be new elections to the Soviet. Shaumyan opposed this, however, and the Bolsheviks handed over power to the new government. A few British units entered Baku shortly afterwards.

As soon as he heard of the revolt Mikoyan hurried to the city, where he received even more alarming news: most of the active leadership of the Baku commune had been arrested. The new administration – the so-called Centro-Caspian Dictatorship – did not last beyond mid-September, however, as the British could not hold back the Turkish advance, and a hasty evacuation was planned. On the very day that the Turkish troops entered Baku Mikoyan managed to liberate Shaumyan and the other Bolsheviks from gaol. Aided by the commander of a small Bolshevik unit, T. M. Amirov, they all managed to board the steamer *Turkmen,* which was already teeming with refugees and soldiers. The ship was bound for Astrakhan, which was under Soviet rule; neither the Dashnaks on board nor the British officers (nor, indeed, many of the soldiers) had the

slightest wish to go there. They succeeded in inciting the crew
to mutiny and diverted the ship to Krasnovodsk, which was
occupied by the British. There the Socialist Revolutionary
authorities arrested all the Bolsheviks. Aided neither by photographs nor by documents – since the Baku Commissars had
none – the authorities were guided by the prison ration cards
that they found on G. N. Korganov, who had been in charge of
Baku gaol, and thus twenty-five men, including Shaumyan,
were singled out. Amirov was thrown in for good measure –
and that was how the legend of the 'Twenty-Six Baku
Commissars' was born. They were taken under guard to the
station at Krasnovodsk, as if they were destined for trial in
Ashkhabad, but they never got that far. On 20 September 1918,
207 kilometres along the railway from Krasnovodsk, they were
all shot. Among them were Communists and Left Socialist
Revolutionaries, Commissars and Shaumyan's personal body-
guard. One of those who was shot was a minor non-Party
employee, but they have all gone down in history.

Anastas Mikoyan's name was not on any prison ration card,
nor was it to be found in the lists of the arrested that
were printed in the Baku newspapers. Other leaders of the
Baku commune who survived were D. V. Kandelaki and E.
Gigoyan. For some time no one in Baku or at the gaol in
Krasnovodsk knew about the executions.

The Turks soon abandoned Azerbaijan; the war ended in an
Allied victory; the Musavatist Government did a deal with the
British; and the workers of Baku went on strike, demanding the
return of Stepan Shaumyan and his comrades. But in February
1919 it was only Mikoyan, Kandelaki and a few other Bolsheviks who came back. Not for another year and a half, by which
time Soviet authority had once more been established in Baku,
were the remains of the executed brought back and ceremoni-
ally buried in one of the town's central squares.

In the autumn of 1919 Mikoyan, as head of the Baku underground Bolshevik organization, went to Moscow to report on
the situation in the Caucasus. There he met Lenin, Stalin and
other leading figures and was made a member of the All-
Russian Central Executive Committee. In the spring of 1920

the Red Army entered Baku and established Soviet power, but Mikoyan did not remain long in the Caucasus. He was suddenly recalled to Moscow and sent with a Central Committee mandate to work in the provincial Party committee of Nizhny-Novgorod, where he met with some distrust among the local leadership.

The situation in both city and province was critical. The 50,000 troops of the garrison were tormented by hunger and cold, and discontent gripped both the peasants and the workers, who had not received wages for months. As an experienced propagandist and agitator, Mikoyan acted with great dispatch and to all intents and purposes was soon running the whole province, which until then had been little more to him than a name in a school geography book. He met Lenin several times, took part in all the Soviet and Party congresses and in May 1922, at the age of 26, was elected to the Central Committee of the Communist Party.

During the course of the two preceding years he had entered Stalin's 'sphere of influence', and even before the Tenth Party Congress of March 1921 he was carrying out confidential missions on his leader's behalf. In the summer of 1922, on Stalin's recommendation, he was appointed secretary of the Central Committee's South-Eastern Bureau. Soon he was running the Northern Caucasus area Party committee, centred on Rostov-on-Don. With a population of some 10 million, the Northern Caucasus embraced the Cossack regions of the Kuban, Terek, Don, Stavropol, Astrakhan and Black Sea provinces, as well as seven national regions, populated by the most diverse ethnic groups. The problems faced by the young Mikoyan were exceptionally complex. The Northern Caucasus had only recently been the scene of fierce civil war battles, and armed bands of Cossacks and tribesmen were still hiding out in the mountains. Nevertheless, under Lenin's New Economic Policy the region gradually recovered from the chaos and became the country's granary once again.

Mikoyan aimed resolutely at closing the gap between the peasants and the Cossacks. The Cossacks were allowed to retain their way of life, their dress, even their own form of military training, and they were encouraged to practise their superb horsemanship (the *dzhigitovka*) and traditional games. Cossack formations were absorbed into the regional units of the Red Army with the slogan 'Make the Cossacks the buttress of Soviet power!' Both the mountain tribesmen and the Cossacks were permitted by the Party regional committee to carry cold steel, as well as to preserve their village administration and budgets. Mikoyan made many speeches calling on the Communists not to destroy churches and mosques and not to take issue with the Cossacks and peasants over religion. He insisted that the rich peasants and big merchants, deprived though they had been of the right to vote, should enjoy to the full the economic rights that had been accorded to them within the framework of the New Economic Policy. In an effort to end the partisan fighting in the region, he declared several amnesties. He took steps to develop the town of Mineralnye Vody and the Black Sea coast as seaside resorts. And as a consequence of all this effort, he acquired a reputation as a competent and experienced administrator and Party leader.

He was on close terms with Stalin by this time and was his staunch ally in the factional struggle against the so-called 'left opposition'. His energy, his Caucasian background and his total loyalty appealed to Stalin, and as early as 1922 Stalin, as General Secretary, began to entrust to him some of the more 'delicate' missions connected with the inner-Party struggle. In July 1926, at the plenum of the Party Central Control Commission, Mikoyan was made a candidate member of the Politburo.

In August 1926 L. B. Kamenev, one of the leaders of the so-called 'left opposition', was relieved of his post as Commissar for Internal and Foreign Trade and packed off to Italy as ambassador. To the surprise of many, the new People's Commissar for Trade was A. I. Mikoyan, at the age of 30 the youngest member of the Politburo and now the youngest People's Commissar.

He put in a great deal of hard work at the Trade Commissariat. The New Economic Policy was in progress; less than five years earlier Lenin had defined trade as the 'main link' that the Bolshevik Party must forge in order to create the complex chain of socialist construction. Lenin's slogan, 'Learn to trade', came as a surprise to many Bolsheviks, who had only recently exchanged their Red Army uniforms for civilian clothes.

The shortage of industrial goods and, connected with it, the problems of grain collection made trade extraordinarily difficult in 1926–27. Mikoyan was decidedly in favour of economic measures to resolve the crisis and equally firmly opposed to the severe treatment of the individual peasant farmers and kulaks that the 'left' was advocating. At the Fifteenth Party Congress he declared that it was essential to emerge from the present crisis 'in the most painless way'. He proposed feeding the towns by means of 'the transfer of goods from the towns to the countryside, even at the cost of denuding the town markets for a few months. If we do not achieve this exchange,' he went on to warn, 'we shall face extraordinary difficulties, which will have an effect on the entire economy.' Stalin did not listen to Mikoyan and the more moderate members of the leadership, however, preferring instead to take extreme measures against the kulaks and a significant section of the peasantry, a course that soon led to the policy of enforced, 'complete' collectivization and the expropriation, deportation and liquidation of the kulaks. Apart from the opposition of many members of the Central Committee, the policy also met with resistance from members of the Politburo, but Mikoyan was not part of this 'right' deviation. As we have seen, he was not in favour of Stalin's plan, leading as it did to devastating results in the countryside, including the grain-rich Northern Caucasus – yet he took Stalin's side.

By the beginning of 1930 the entire system of trade was in chaos. Food collection assumed the character of requisitioning, as purchase prices were no longer related to the actual cost of agricultural produce. Inflation took off, and paper money quickly lost its value. The food shortage in the towns led to the introduction of strict regulation and rationing. Severe famine raged in many rural areas, and millions died. Workers and employees were allocated rations according to the work that they did, the posts that they held and other considerations. Once again trade began to give way to barter, through which the cities kept themselves supplied with food, while the countryside acquired industrial goods. The new situation corresponded neither to the methods nor indeed the name of the Trade Commissariat that Mikoyan headed, and in 1930 it was reorganized as the People's Commissariat of Supply. For the overwhelming majority of the population in the early 1930s, however, the supply was extremely meagre, and a gloomy joke circulated: 'We've got no meat, no milk, no butter, no flour, no soap, but we have got Mikoyan' (in Russian the words in the list all start with 'm').

Nevertheless, in one commercial venture Mikoyan was very successful, and that was the sale abroad of part of the collections of the Hermitage and the Museum of Modern Western Art (now called the Pushkin Museum) and of countless precious objects that had been confiscated from the Russian imperial family and the aristocracy. At the beginning of the first Five-Year Plan the USSR was suffering from an acute shortage of hard currency with which to pay for imported equipment. The drop in agricultural production cut the country's export potential to the bone. The idea arose of selling some paintings by such old masters as Rembrandt, Rubens, Titian, Raphael, Van Dyck and Poussin, as well as goldwork and jewellery, furniture from the Tsar's palaces, some of which had belonged to the French king, and a part of Nicolas I's library. A. V. Lunacharsky, who was Commissar for Education and ran the country's museums, was wholly opposed to these sales, but he was overruled by the Politburo.

The sale of the Hermitage treasures turned out to be no simple matter, thanks to the protests of leading Russian émigrés; and the first auction, which was held in Germany, yielded poor results. There were to be problems for the Soviet Union in France too, since there a number of the *objets d'art* put up for sale became objects of litigation instead. Then Mikoyan concluded his first big deal with the famous Armenian multi-millionaire, Gulbenkian, and the Americans started to buy his pictures, the biggest deals being those made with the fabulously wealthy former Secretary to the US Treasury, Andrew Mellon. Sales continued on a smaller scale until 1936 and yielded the USSR a total of some $100 million.

Stalin had such complete faith in Mikoyan at this time that when V. R. Menzhinsky, the head of the GPU (State Security), fell ill, Stalin proposed that he take his place. But Mikoyan was not especially keen to drop commerce and supply in order to take charge of the state penal system, and the appointment was not made.

Mikoyan took no direct part in the punitive actions of the collectivization and enforced requisitions of 1930–33, though he did sanction the arrest of many non-Party specialists and experts, frequently those employed as his own Commissariat senior staff, who were slanderously accused of sabotage. He may not have been the instigator of these acts of terror, but nor did he ever come out in protest against them. An illustration of his pragmatism was the case of M. P. Yakubovich, who ran the industrial goods administration in the Trade Commissariat. The supply plans that he compiled were studied by Mikoyan with meticulous thoroughness and later confirmed by the governing board of the Commissariat. The basic supply control data were even examined by the Politburo. Then, in response to mass protests by workers, Mikoyan gave instructions that supplies to certain towns should be increased at the expense of others. Yakubovich reminded him that the Politburo had already approved the supply dispositions, but Mikoyan cited Stalin's personal instructions and Yakubovich submitted. Soon, however, outbursts of discontent erupted in still more towns, and an article duly appeared in *Pravda* accusing Yakubovich and his department of sabotage. He was arrested. At his first interrogation he demanded that Mikoyan be summoned as a witness, but his interrogator merely smiled. 'Are you crazy?' he asked. 'Do you think we'd call a People's Commissar of the USSR as a witness for you?' Yakubovich was sentenced and spent more than twenty-five years in prisons and labour camps.

The political and economic crisis of 1928–33 began to subside as the wounds inflicted on the country and the people by the 'revolution from above' gradually healed. At the same time the enormous effort that had been expended on building up industry during that period began to bear fruit. More slowly than heavy industry, light industry and food manufacture were also developing. In 1934 an independent Commissariat of Food Production was created, with Mikoyan at its head. In good years there were no shortages of foodstuffs in the USSR, but the food industry was very backward, and there was practically no public dining-rooms or canteens. Mikoyan went on a lengthy trip to the USA to see for himself the different varieties and techniques of food production, and it was thanks to his initiative and efficient leadership that under the second Five-Year Plan new processes were introduced into food production in the USSR. The innovations included canning, improved sugar-production techniques and advances in the manufacture of confectionery, bakery products, salami and sausages, fats and so on. He also pushed for the rapid development of refrigeration and the production of all kinds of ice-cream. Thanks to him, there was a significant increase in the production of chops in the Soviet Union – the best chops are often still called 'Mikoyans' today.

The entire liqueur and vodka industry in the USSR was also under Mikoyan's control. Speaking at the First Congress of Stakhanovites (record-breaking workers) in November 1935 he said:

> In 1935 less vodka was sold than in 1934, and in 1934, despite its superior quality, less was sold than in 1933. This is the only branch of production under the Food Production Commissariat that is not progressing but declining, to the great distress of our vodka-industry workers. But let us not worry about the fact that our vodka makers are concerned. Comrade Stalin warned us a long time ago that as the cultural level of the country rose, so the level of vodka consumption would fall and the importance of cinema and radio would grow.[1]

But the vodka makers were not distressed for long. Today we have not only radio and cinema but also television, and the production of vodka, having risen steadily through the 1960s and 1970s, now exceeds the pre-war level by a very large margin.

In the early 1930s Mikoyan was instrumental in bringing out the first Soviet cookery book, called *The Book of Healthy and Tasty Food*. It opens with Stalin's words, 'Life has become better, life has become merrier', and for each section of the book Mikoyan found an appropriate epigraph. Thus at the head of the section on fish dishes is the following little vignette: 'Comrade Stalin once asked, "Tell me, Comrade Mikoyan, can one buy live fish in the Moscow shops?" "No, Comrade Stalin," I replied. "Well, one used to be able to," he said. And now nineteen shops in Moscow sell live fish!'

As an administrator Mikoyan was generally very considerate towards his subordinates. When he was in a good mood he might give them oranges from a bowl on his table. But he was also one of 'Stalin's Commissars' and, like Kaganovich, when he was in a bad mood he was capable of throwing files of letters, signed or unsigned, in their faces. That was not all. In 1935 he became a fully-fledged member of the Politburo and, in 1937, deputy chairman of the Council of People's Commissars. Some of his close friends and relatives maintain that he had no hand in the repressions and terror of the 1930s, though he did not openly protest against them. Unfortunately, these assertions are not altogether realistic.

Of course, Mikoyan was not as active or aggressive as, say, Kaganovich. Moreover, as a member of the Politburo he could not actually decline to take part in the terror, but nor could he refuse to bear his share of responsibility for Politburo decisions that resulted in the terrible events of that decade. Stalin did not merely sign the lists of those intended for 'liquidation' presented to him by N. I. Yezhov; he also passed them round to the other Politburo members. Furthermore, People's Commissars had to sanction the arrest of leading members of their own staff, so it is difficult to believe that Mikoyan knew nothing about the repression of many of the top personnel in the food industry and in commerce. By contrast, G. K. Ordzhonikidze, who had tried to protect his staff, was driven to suicide in early 1937. He had been a friend of Mikoyan, who had named the youngest of his five sons, Sergo, after him. Twenty years later, speaking at the Red Proletarian Factory, Mikoyan told the story of how Stalin had summoned him after Ordzhonikidze's death and had said, threateningly: 'That story of the shooting of the twenty-six Baku Commissars and how only one of them, you, managed to stay alive – it's all pretty vague and confused.

And you've never wanted us to try to clear it up, have you, Anastas Ivanovich?'

Living under the constant threat that he might be accused of betraying his comrades in the Baku commune, even Ordzhonikidze's solution was not an option for Mikoyan. So he submitted to Stalin. At the February–March 1937 Central Committee plenum he was put in charge of a commission whose brief was to decide the fate of Bukharin and Rykov. Its terms of reference were brief and to the point: 'Arrest. Try. Shoot.'

In the autumn of that year Mikoyan went to Armenia with Malenkov, who was not yet even a member of the Central Committee, in order to 'purge' the Party and state apparatus of any local 'enemies of the people'. This was a vicious campaign of terror, as a result of which thousands of entirely innocent regional personnel perished. At the end of 1937 the republic's newspaper, *Kommunist,* wrote:

> On the great Stalin's orders, Comrade Mikoyan rendered a great service to the Bolsheviks of Armenia in unmasking and rooting out the enemies of the Armenian people – the despicable bandits Amatuni, Guloyan, Akopov *et al,* – who were forcing their way to the leadership with the aim of handing over the Armenian people to a cabal of landowners and capitalists.
>
> With passionate hatred for all enemies of socialism, Comrade Mikoyan ably assisted the Armenian people, and on the great Stalin's orders he personally helped the workers and peasants of Armenia to unmask and destroy their base enemies, the Trotskyist–Bukharinist, Dashnak–Nationalist spies, who were wrecking workers' and peasants' Armenia. . . .
>
> It was Mikoyan who, on the orders of the great Stalin, exposed and threw out the workers' sworn enemies, the Trotskyists and Dashnaks, Amatuni, Akopov, Guloyan, Zhugdusi and other riff-raff.[2]

It was also Mikoyan who represented the Politburo at a ceremony of the NKVD celebrating the twentieth anniversary of the Cheka–GPU–NKVD, the organs of repression. In his speech he reviled the 'enemies of the people', who at that time included a majority of the Party Central Committee membership, and he said of 'Stalin's Commissar' Yezhov:

Learn the Stalin way to work from Comrade Yezhov, just as he
learned, and will continue to learn, from Comrade Stalin
himself. Comrade Yezhov has created in the NKVD a wonder-
ful backbone of Chekists. He has trained them in true Bolshevik
manner in the spirit of Dzerzhinsky [the first chairman of the
Cheka] and of our Party.[3]

He ended his speech with the exclamation: 'The NKVD has
worked gloriously during this time!' – he was talking about
1937. Someone who happened to be present at the meeting
recalled decades later:

Mikoyan read his speech dressed in a dark Caucasian shirt and
belt. I couldn't make out what he was saying, no doubt because
of his thick accent. Stalin was not on the platform. Budyonny
arrived very late, and the meeting was frequently interrupted by
ovations, and even by some woman who shouted out something. Then there was another ovation – that was when Stalin
stood up in his box – and it did not die down until he had
vanished again. But probably the most uproarious greeting was
that given to their favourite 'Stalinist Commissar', Yezhov.
He stood, with his shock of thick black hair, eyes cast down and
a sheepish grin on his face, as if he wasn't sure that he deserved
such a rapturous reception.[4]

It should be acknowledged, however, that Mikoyan did help
a number of people, both those who had not yet been arrested
and the relations of his arrested comrades, promising them
'at the earliest opportunity' to help to free their husbands, sons
or fathers. For example, I. Kh. Bagramyan, who would later
distinguish himself during the Second World War, was still
studying at the Staff Academy in 1937, when a campaign of
denunciation was raging there and super-vigilance was the
order of the day. No doubt because of his Armenian origins,
Bagramyan was accused of belonging to the Dashnaks, and he
expected to be arrested any day, though he had documentary
proof that the charge was false. On the advice of friends,
he wrote to Mikoyan, who came to the aid of his countryman,
and Bagramyan was rehabilitated.

Another case was that of A. V. Snegov, who had been a

friend of Mikoyan in the early 1920s, when they were young provincial committee secretaries in Nizhny-Novgorod and Poltava respectively. Snegov was arrested in Leningrad, and, after cruel torture, sentenced to be shot. His 'accomplices' had nearly all been shot when Snegov was suddenly reprieved. Yezhov had already been removed from his post, and news had come in of the arrest of the head of Leningrad NKVD, L. M. Zakovsky. A few days later Snegov was released and given a certificate of rehabilitation. He went to see A. A. Zhdanov, secretary of the Leningrad Party committee, in the Smolny and told him at length what was happening in the corridors of power at the NKVD. Zhdanov, it seems, was even better informed than Snegov and advised him to leave Leningrad at once and to try as hard as possible to get reinstated in the Party.

Snegov left for Moscow, where he paid a visit to A. A. Andreyev, who was at that time heading a commission of inquiry into Yezhov's activities. For nearly five hours Snegov told Andreyev what was going on behind the walls of the Leningrad NKVD. But his information was not news to Andreyev either, as he himself had played an active part in many of the campaigns of terror of 1937–38. Snegov also reported his release to Molotov, who coolly took note of it, and also to M. I. Kalinin, who said, 'Well, well, you've really been through it. Why not drop in some time?'

Snegov then telephoned Mikoyan, who asked him to come round straight away and listened to his story with great attention. When he heard about L. M. Zakovsky's execution he said, 'One swine the less', but he was sorry to hear about the suicide of M. I. Litvin, a Party worker who had been posted to the NKVD and had shot himself at the end of a week, leaving a note in which he had written that he had no desire to take part in the destruction of the Party cadres. Mikoyan advised Snegov not to go to the Party Control Commission. He gave him a rest-home warrant for himself and his wife, together with a little money, and advised them to take a holiday instead. But Snegov persisted, so Mikoyan finally rang A. G. Shkiryatov at the Party Control Commission and asked him to settle Snegov's problem as soon as possible. Shkiryatov claimed to be 'rather concerned' about the case, and when Snegov arrived at the Control Commission he was asked to wait in the lobby for a short while. Less than half an hour later into the lobby marched four KNVD men bearing not Snegov's Party membership card but an order for his arrest, signed by Beria. Shkiryatov was one of Beria's men, and apparently Beria remembered Snegov and had hated him since the time he had worked in the Caucasus in 1930–31.[5]

In 1937–38 Stalin's fearful machine of terror destroyed the greater part of the Party, soviet, military and economic personnel in the top and middle ranks. The country could not remain without leadership, however, so new men took the places of those who had been liquidated or incarcerated. For many people this was a time of astonishingly swift promotion. The story of A. N. Kosygin illustrates this point very well.

Having spent some years as a modest worker in the consumers' co-operatives system in Siberia, Kosygin entered the Leningrad Textile Institute in 1930 and, on completion of his training there in 1935, was sent as a workshop foreman to the A. I. Zhelyabov Textile Factory. As early as 1937 he was appointed manager of the October Spinning and Weaving Works; in 1938 he was running the industrial section of the Leningrad Party regional committee (obkom); and in the same year he was appointed chairman of the Leningrad city soviet executive committee. It was at this time that he was spotted by Mikoyan, who was impressed by his youth and energy, and when in the following year, 1939, the decision was taken to create an All-Union People's Commissariat for the Textile Industry, Mikoyan recommended to Stalin a vigorous young leader in Leningrad who knew all about textile manufacture. Stalin accepted the nomination, and Kosygin was summoned to Moscow. Before he had left Leningrad railway station, he knew he had been appointed Soviet People's Commissar for the Textile Industry.

In 1939–40, as People's Commissar for Foreign Trade, Mikoyan held talks with German economic delegations and ensured that the agreements were fulfilled punctiliously. Although delivery dates for equipment from Germany fell behind as early as 1940, the trains carrying food and raw

materials from the USSR to Germany went on running
practically up to the day of the German invasion, 21 June 1941.
The war changed all that, as it changed Mikoyan's duties.

Even before the war, while he was in control of the whole
sphere of trade, supply and the production of consumer goods
and foodstuffs, Mikoyan had announced: 'We can now say that
when the Red Army demands food supplies in time of war, it
will receive adequate quantities of condensed milk, coffee and
cocoa, canned meat and chicken, sweets, jam and many other
things in which our country is rich.'[6] Of course, supplies to the
Red Army during the war years were not exactly abundant, but
they were adequate. Soon after the outbreak of the war
Mikoyan was heading a Committee for the Supply of Food and
Clothing to the Red Army, and in 1942 he was appointed to the
State Defence Committee, the highest authority in the land
during wartime. His contribution to the organization of
supplies was so evident that in 1943, while the war was still
raging, he was made a Hero of Socialist Labour. Soon after the
outbreak of the war Mikoyan was appointed to the Council for
Evacuation, which was headed by N. M. Shvernik. This body
was charged with the enormous task of moving millions of
workers and thousands of industrial enterprises to the eastern
and southern regions of the country. By the beginning of 1943
something like 25 million people had been evacuated. As the
Red Army began its advance westwards, Mikoyan joined the
committee formed for the economic reconstruction of territories liberated from Nazi occupation.

However, we should note not only the services that Mikoyan
rendered during the war but also the fact that, as a member
of the Politburo and State Defence Committee, he shared
responsibility for all the decisions either taken or approved by
those two supreme bodies. In particular, I have in mind the
deportation of entire nationalities from their own territories to
so-called 'special settlements' in the east. Such was the fate of
the Volga Germans and all Soviet citizens of German origin at
the outbreak of the war, of many of the nationalities and ethnic
groups of the Northern Caucasus in 1943 and of the Crimean
Tatars in 1945. In each case the question of whether one or
another national administrative entity should be liquidated and

its population deported was submitted by Stalin for approval by the Politburo and the State Defence Committee – and in fairness we should note that Mikoyan's position differed, however insignificantly, from that taken by the rest of the leadership.

In 1951 the émigré Menshevik journal *Sotsialisticheskii Vestnik* (*Socialist Messenger*) printed the testimony of a certain Colonel Tokayev, an Ossetian who had evidently escaped to the West at the end of, or immediately after, the war.[7] According to Tokayev, the decision to liquidate the Chechen–Ingush Autonomous Soviet Socialist Republic (ASSR) was taken at a joint meeting of the Politburo and the State Defence Committee on 11 February 1943, where two views emerged. Molotov, A. A. Zhdanov, N. A. Voznesensky and A. A. Andreyev were in favour of publicly liquidating the Chechen–Ingush ASSR and deporting all Chechens and Ingushes from the Northern Caucasus forthwith, while Voroshilov, Kaganovich, Khrushchev, Kalinin and Beria proposed delaying the deportations until the Northern Caucasus had been liberated from German occupation. Stalin sided with this view. Only Mikoyan, though agreeing in principle that the Chechens and Ingushes should be deported, expressed concern that the deportations would damage the reputation of the USSR abroad.[8]

After the war was over Mikoyan continued as deputy chairman of the Council of Ministers and Minister of Foreign Trade. But apart from the problems raised by trade and light industry, he also found himself burdened again with the responsibility of solving extremely 'delicate' questions – for example, that of the case of the former Commissar for the Aviation Industry, M. Kaganovich (see pp. 132–3). Mikoyan was, of course, perfectly aware of the campaign of repression that was in progress against a large group of Leningrad leaders, and also of the arrests that had taken place in Moscow of A. A. Kuznetsov, M. I. Rodionov, A. A. Voznesensky and N. A. Voznesensky, the chairman of Gosplan, who had also often acted as chairman of the Council of Ministers. Mikoyan had been accustomed to co-ordinating much of his work with N. A. Voznesensky, and they had only rarely approached Stalin, who did not like taking part in the Council of Ministers.

In 1968, during the 'Prague Spring', documents were published that showed that in 1949–51, after the rift with Yugoslavia and when a wave of terror swept through the People's Democracies of Eastern Europe, it was Mikoyan who, in talks on Stalin's behalf with Klement Gottwald, President of Czechoslovakia, insisted on the removal and arrest of Rudolf Slansky, Secretary-General of the Czech Communist Party.

Terror had touched Mikoyan's own family somewhat earlier as part of a tragedy that struck the children of certain highly placed figures towards the end of the war. The Soviet diplomat K. A. Umansky, who had been appointed ambassador to Mexico, had intended to take his whole family with him. However, the son of the Aviation Industry Minister, A. I. Shakhurin, was in love with Umansky's daughter and forbade her to go. She was defiant, so he shot her and then killed himself. In the course of the investigation that ensued, it transpired that the 'Kremlin children' played at 'government', electing Commissars and Ministers and even their own head of government. The prosecuting authorities found nothing criminal in all this, but Stalin insisted on a review of the case, as a result of which Mikoyan's two sons, the youngest, Sergo, and an older boy, Vano, were arrested and exiled briefly, returning shortly after the end of the war. During a meeting of the Politburo Stalin suddenly asked Mikoyan what his younger sons were doing. 'They're at school,' Mikoyan answered. 'They have earned the right to study in a Soviet school,' Stalin affirmed in his typically banal and malicious way.

After the war Stalin often invited Politburo members, Ministers and senior army officers to dine with him at his dacha and to watch movies with him. His wife had committed suicide in 1932, and he never married again; as his visitors never brought their wives along, the company was almost always entirely male, though occasionally Stalin's daughter, Svetlana, was present. Stalin would wind up the gramophone, put on a record and invite everyone to dance, something they all did badly but in which they could hardly refuse to participate, especially as Stalin himself would sometimes start the dancing. The only man who knew how to dance at all was Mikoyan – except that whatever music was playing, he would execute the same steps, those of a basic kind of Caucasian folk-dance.

From 1951 on Mikoyan was invited to the dacha less and less frequently. Nor was he summoned to meetings of the Polit-buro, and in 1952, at the Nineteenth Party Congress, he was not even included in the Presidium of the Congress, though naturally the speech he gave was full of praise for Stalin. He was elected to the Party Central Committee and also to the enlarged new Presidium of the Central Committee that was created in place of the old Politburo that Stalin abolished on that occasion, but he was not made a member of the Bureau, an inner group of the Presidium that was in effect the old Politburo under a different name. At the plenum session of the Congress Stalin attacked Molotov and Mikoyan and indicated his lack of trust in them. They defended themselves, but they were considered by many to be doomed men. None of this, however, prevented Mikoyan from working as energetically as ever in the Council of Ministers.

Immediately after Stalin's death the Central Committee Pres-idium and Secretariat and the Council of Ministers were sharply reduced in size. Once again Mikoyan found a secure footing for himself in the highest reaches of the Party and state machine. Official announcements at that time listed the leaders not in alphabetical order but according to their position in the Party hierarchy. Khrushchev was fifth, after Malenkov, Molotov, Beria and Kaganovich, while Mikoyan occupied eighth place, following Voroshilov and N. A. Bulganin.

In the struggle for power that developed soon after Stalin's death, Mikoyan remained somewhat aloof. Khrushchev in-formed him of his plan to arrest Beria at the last moment, just before the Presidium was due to meet, but Mikoyan took a cautious position and did not rush to join the conspiracy. As Khrushchev later recalled, 'Mikoyan listened, made a few remarks, but then announced that Beria was not a hopeless case and that he could function in the collective leadership.' Mikoyan's stance greatly worried Khrushchev, who shared his concern with Malenkov. But it was too late to retreat, and the meeting was duly opened. Khrushchev spoke first, explaining in detail why it was necessary to dismiss Beria. He was followed by Bulganin, who also called for Beria's dismissal. All the rest supported Khrushchev except Mikoyan, who put his own point of view; while he agreed with many of the charges that had been made against Beria, he nevertheless believed that Beria would 'take our criticisms to heart and reform himself, that he wasn't a hopeless case, and that he could still be useful in the collective leadership'.[9]

Once Beria had been removed, however, Mikoyan gave Khrushchev his support in all important matters. He helped in the return and rehabilitation of many of his old friends and colleagues, some of whom had held high posts in the Party and state apparatus, and in 1954 he went to Yugoslavia to prepare the ground for the visit by the Soviet delegation, which was designed to foster reconciliation.

Shortly before the Twentieth Party Congress Khrushchev proposed that the question of Stalin's crimes should be debated there. Nearly all the members of the Presidium were against such a move; Mikoyan neither supported nor opposed Khrushchev on this occasion. Khrushchev returned to the question while the Congress was in progress, however, declaring that he would ask the delegates themselves to decide. The Presidium finally agreed, after painful debate, that Khrushchev should give his speech on Stalin at the final session of the Congress, after the elections to the Central Committee had taken place. But a full ten days before Khrushchev made his famous 'secret speech' it was none other than Mikoyan himself who, quite unexpectedly but confidently and in some detail, raised the question of Stalin's abuse of power. 'In the course of nearly twenty years,' he said, 'to all intents and purposes we had no collective leadership, and the cult of personality flourished.' He attacked the many mistakes that Stalin had made in foreign policy, and he declared that Stalin's *History of the Communist Party (Short Course)* gave an unsatisfactory account of the Party's history and that his last work, *Economic Problems of Socialism in the USSR,* was full of mistakes. He then went on to speak warmly of 'Comrades S. V. Kosior and V. A. Antonov-Ovseyenko', who had been purged and had perished at the end of the 1930s, and then, in more general terms, he

declared that there were no real Marxist works on the history of
the civil war and that many Party workers of the civil war
period had been maligned as 'enemies of the people' and
'saboteurs'.[10] Mikoyan's long speech was the central event of
the Congress and provoked lively commentary in the international press. The former correspondent of the Italian
Communist newspaper *Unità,* Giuseppe Boffa, described
Mikoyan's speech thus:

> Mikoyan spoke passionately and quickly, half-swallowing his
> words, as if he were afraid that he would not have enough time
> to say everything he wanted. It was very hard to follow the
> speech, but even a few phrases at the beginning of it were
> enough to seize everyone's attention. Absolute silence reigned.
> Stalin's name occurred only once in the whole speech. But the
> critical remarks he made about the dead leader were almost
> ferocious in their categorical certainty. There had been nothing
> in the preceding speeches to match this outright condemnation.
> When he finished speaking the hall seethed with excitement.
> Nobody listened to the next speaker.[11]

After the Twentieth Congress Mikoyan organized about a
hundred commissions whose remit was to visit all the labour
camps and other places of detention and to carry out a rapid
review of the charges against all political prisoners. P. A.
Rudenko, the public prosecutor, whose apparatus was dealing
very slowly with the matter of the victims' reinstatement,
protested at first against these commissions, invested as they
were with powers of rehabilitation and clemency, but he gave
way when Mikoyan intervened.

Yet by then Mikoyan himself, when he spoke in front of the
general public, was calling for care and moderation in the
criticism of Stalin. At a meeting of Moscow intellectuals, when
some of the writers present advanced heated and cogent
arguments for widening and deepening the criticism of the 'cult
of personality', Mikoyan lost his temper and shouted at one of
them, 'Do you want to unleash the elements?'[12] And Svetlana
Alliluyeva relates in her book *Just One Year* that during a visit to
Mikoyan, after the Twentieth Congress, he presented her with
the gift of a beautifully made medallion bearing a portrait of
Stalin.

During the October 1956 political crisis in Poland, Mikoyan was the first to arrive in Warsaw to assess the nature and scale of the events, and he was also in Budapest in early November while the uprising was in progress and new Party and state machinery was being created to run Hungary.

Mikoyan was firmly on Khrushchev's side at the June 1957 plenum of the Central Committee, even though their group was at first in the minority. He was the only member of Stalin's original Politburo to support Khrushchev, but after the plenum he was to be permanently one of the three or four most influential people in the Party and Government. He often carried out important diplomatic missions; he made official and unofficial trips to India, Pakistan, China and other countries, and at the beginning of 1959 he went to the USA to open the Soviet exhibition in New York and to hold talks about Khrushchev's future American visit. He gave many successful speeches – on one occasion he was asked if he was going to run for Senate.

Khrushchev sometimes called in Mikoyan to settle ideological problems, such as the case of Academician A. M. Deborin. Deborin was one of the best-known Soviet philosophers of the 1920s and a prominent organizer of the teaching of philosophy. He created his school of dialecticians, the 'Deborin school', which led a vigorous debate against the so-called 'mechanists'. On Stalin's initiative, Deborin's school was at first smeared as a group of 'Menshevizing idealists', and then, at the end of the 1930s, nearly all the Deborinists were arrested. Deborin himself was left at large, but he was given no opportunity to speak or publish. Mikoyan, of course, had not the slightest idea what a 'Menshevizing idealist' was, nor did he attempt to delve into the intricate philosophical debates of the 1920s or try to obtain a formal resolution of the Central Committee on philosophical problems. Instead he gave the order to publish a number of Deborin's large works on the history of sociology and philosophy, written originally in the 1930s and 40s, and also saw to it that Deborin was given the chance to supervise a group of postgraduates. And when Khrushchev received Solzhenitsyn's manuscript of *One Day in the Life of Ivan Denisovich* from A. T.

Tvardovsky, the editor of the journal *Novy Mir* (*New World*), he not only read it himself but also passed it on to Mikoyan for comment. Mikoyan was in favour of its publication, and Khrushchev submitted it to the Presidium for consideration.

Some of Mikoyan's jobs were more taxing. In 1961, for instance, he had to fly to the Chechen–Ingush ASSR to resolve clashes that had erupted in the town of Grozny between the Russian population and the Chechens and Ingushes who had returned home from deportation. He managed to quell the troubles without bloodshed or recourse to mass arrests. On the other hand, a year later, when the citizens of Novocherkassk were restive because of the poor food supply and increases in the price of meat, milk, butter and cheese, a workers' demonstration was quashed with the help of troops and many arrests; Mikoyan and M. A. Suslov were both there at the time. In private conversations later Mikoyan blamed Suslov for the bloodshed and claimed that he personally had thought it feasible to arrange talks with workers' representatives. Whether this was true or not cannot be established.

Mikoyan was to play his most important role in world diplomacy at the end of 1962, during the Cuban missile crisis, when for a few days the USSR and the USA came to within a hair's breadth of war. There had been no more dangerous time since the end of the Second World War.

The crisis was provoked by the installation on Cuba of Soviet medium-range missiles equipped with nuclear warheads. Khrushchev had embarked on this venture in an attempt simultaneously to tilt the worldwide strategic balance in the Soviet Union's favour and to even up each side's chances of making a nuclear strike at short range. The Soviet Union was surrounded on all sides by American military bases, and American aircraft carrying atomic bombs ceaselessly patrolled the Soviet coastlines. Located in close proximity to the USA, Cuba would become one of the most important of the USSR's military bases if the gamble were successful and would help to correct the imbalance of power. Khrushchev and his advisers misjudged the likely response, however. The American failure to topple Fidel Castro's regime by invasion did not deter the USA from making numerous other attempts; and when President Kennedy was shown reconnaissance photographs, from which it was plain that the USSR had begun to station and assemble surface-to-surface missiles on Cuba, his reaction was tough. The US National Security Council took the decision to use all available means to prevent the completion of the installations, which would have placed on Cuban soil enough Soviet missiles to wipe dozens of American towns off the face of the earth. Refraining from immediate intervention and the bombardment of the island, which many American politicians and generals were advocating, President Kennedy decided to launch a military attack on Cuba only in the event that diplomacy failed to bring about a rapid and successful outcome. A quarter of a million troops and 90,000 Marines were poised ready for the campaign. The US Army, Navy and Air Force were on red alert all over the world, and, with the approval of the Western countries, the USA declared a naval blockade of Cuba.

The reaction of the United States alarmed Khrushchev. He did not want war, but events were moving inexorably in the direction of military conflict. In response to a US strike against Cuba, the USSR could occupy West Berlin, but that move too was almost bound to lead to war with the West. He attempted to formulate a compromise, but Fidel Castro was taking a very hard line, objecting to the withdrawal of the missiles and even going so far as to surround the missile sites with Cuban troops.

What was needed was a capable, experienced and wise mediator. The choice fell upon Mikoyan, who had already spent quite some time in Cuba in 1959, when he had negotiated the USSR's first important agreements on trade and economic aid to the young republic, and who had also opened the first Soviet exhibition there.

Mikoyan flew straight to Cuba on receiving his new assignment. The importance of the role he played in the crisis cannot be exaggerated. Working day and night, he went over every kind of proposal to end the crisis and conducted extremely complicated talks. His most difficult task was to persuade Castro to accept the Soviet proposals, and he managed even that. He also had to pre-empt any precipitate action on the part of Khrushchev, who at first gave orders to speed up the assembly of the missiles at their sites. Work on the launch pads went on round the clock. At the same time the rapid unloading of military cargoes and the assembly of Il-28 strategic bombers was proceeding apace. Denouncing the naval blockade as 'banditry' and 'the folly of degenerate imperialism', Khrushchev issued orders to the captains of Soviet ships, as they were approaching the blockade zone, to ignore it and to hold course for the Cuban ports. The situation worsened from day to day, if not from hour to hour. The break came on 26–7 October 1962, when for the first time Khrushchev publicly acknowledged the existence of offensive missiles on Cuba and when it also became clear that the US response was not mere bluff. Khrushchev agreed to dismantle the missiles in exchange for the lifting of the blockade and a US undertaking not to invade Cuba. Kennedy accepted this proposal. There was also a secret agreement that the USA would remove her missiles from Turkish territory and reduce the establishment at her base at Guantanamo in Cuba.

The Soviet missiles were soon dismantled and shipped out, and the Soviet Union agreed that US and United Nations experts could inspect the Soviet vessels. The crisis had been averted with the minimum loss of Soviet prestige. Indeed, Soviet–American relations improved if anything, a development that led in 1963 to the signing of the partial nuclear test-ban treaty, an extremely important measure in limiting the arms race and protecting the environment.

Acting mainly behind the scenes and as a mediator between Khrushchev, Kennedy and Castro, Mikoyan had played a very big part in the Cuban crisis, which was not without danger. During one of his flights to Washington first one of the engines in the Boeing caught fire, then a second. Panic broke out in the cabin, but Mikoyan, who was with a group of Soviet experts that included one of his own sons, instructed everyone to remain calm. 'Behave like men,' he said, and continued to chat to his companions about anything but their likely sudden death. Luckily, the crew managed to deal with the situation, and the plane landed safely.

Mikoyan's wife, Ashkhen, with whom he had lived in peace

and contentment for more than forty years, died during the Cuban crisis. He could not attend her funeral, and she was buried by three of their sons – one had perished in the war and another was with Mikoyan in Cuba – their many grandchildren and Mikoyan's youngest brother, Artem, the famous Academician and Air Force general who had designed many supersonic fighters [the MiG is named after its designers, Mikoyan and Gurevich].

Mikoyan did not return to Moscow immediately after the Cuban crisis but spent several days in the USA, where he had talks with President Kennedy. And just one year later he was back in the USA, at the head of a Soviet delegation, to attend the funeral of the President, assassinated by a sniper's bullet in Dallas.

When L. I. Brezhnev became second secretary of the Party Central Committee in 1963 and the question arose of the appointment of his successor as chairman of the Presidium of the Supreme Soviet, the choice was Mikoyan, who duly took up the post in July 1964. A month later he signed the decree rehabilitating the Volga Germans and other citizens of German ethnic origin who had been illegally condemned and deported to the eastern zones of the USSR in 1942. The Autonomous German Volga Republic was not reinstated, however, and many problems faced by Soviet Germans were not resolved.

Khrushchev discussed with Mikoyan plans to reorganize the Supreme Soviet and to widen its functions in the higher reaches of the power structure; in particular he wished to make its sessions longer and more relevant. It was Khrushchev's idea at that time to turn it into a sort of socialist Parliament, and he thought Mikoyan the right man to carry out the reform, though in fact it was never even begun. Moreover, only three months after he had been appointed as head of government, Mikoyan signed the order dismissing Khrushchev from his posts as chairman of the Council of Ministers and First Secretary of the Party Central Committee, which were now given to A. N. Kosygin and L. I. Brezhnev respectively.

Reports appeared in the Western press to the effect that Mikoyan had played a prominent part in the plot to oust

Khrushchev, that in early October 1964 he had gone with Khrushchev to the south in order to divert his attention and to frustrate any possible counter-moves that he might make. These reports were plainly inventions. It is true that in October 1964 Mikoyan was on holiday not far from where Khrushchev was staying, and it is true that they were both summoned to Moscow together to attend the Central Committee Presidium meeting; but all the facts indicate that Mikoyan was the one Presidium member who did not take part in the preliminary discussions about dismissing Khrushchev, and when the enlarged Presidium met in the afternoon of 13 October Mikoyan was, once again, the only man to defend Khrushchev. 'Khrushchev and his peace policy are important assets for the Party,' he declared, 'and they are not to be scorned.' Late that night, during an interval in the proceedings, Khrushchev went home to take a rest. He recognized that it was useless to fight any longer, he told Mikoyan, who was the first person he telephoned, and he made up his mind to write a letter of resignation.

Mikoyan was probably the only member of the Central Committee Presidium who, when speaking of the results of the October plenum, referred to Khrushchev's merits and not only to his shortcomings. At a Party meeting at the Red Proletarian Factory in December 1964, for instance, he said:

We cannot deny Khrushchev's great services – in the struggle for peace, in eliminating the consequences of the cult of personality, in the expansion of socialist democracy, in the preparation and conduct of the most important Party Congresses . . . and in getting the Party programme accepted. But the further he went, the more the mistakes and shortcomings in his work and his leadership accumulated. These shortcomings were largely the consequence of his physical condition – the effects of age and his sclerotic state. He became irritable, fussy, volatile, restless. He could not sit still and work for more than three hours at a stretch; he was always on the move, going on trips. He had a tendency to improvise in everything he did, to make decisions on the job. . . . His irritability and intolerance of criticism were traits that even those comrades whom he had advanced to leading posts did not find attractive. When things were going

badly in agriculture Khrushchev did not try to discover the
objective causes; instead he looked for solutions by chivvying
individuals and moving them around from job to job. . . .
He had an organizational itch, a need to keep on reorganizing
things. I think we treated Khrushchev according to the rules.
The Presidium has remained practically unchanged. It includes
three generations: the old, which means Shvernik (aged 76) and
myself (69); the middle-aged, Brezhnev (58), Kosygin (60) and
Podgorny (61); and the young, consisting of Shelepin, though at
46 he is not that young. So it is a good deed that we have done.
The leadership of the Central Committee now functions in a
normal atmosphere. Everyone can express himself freely, not
like before, when only Khrushchev spoke. Now we have
achieved a real Leninist leadership. The Central Committee has
enormous experience, and changes will be made for the benefit
of the people, who will soon feel their effects in practice.

The post of chairman of the Presidium of the Supreme Soviet
is not a very onerous one. Nevertheless, Mikoyan was not
merely the formal head of government. With his great experience, his knowledge and expertise, his flexible mind and his
prestige as the last of the Leninist old guard, he was an
enormously influential member of the new 'collective leadership'. He was someone to be reckoned with. As he was so
clever and so cautious, he would, it seemed, give no cause for
his removal from office. And yet a cause was found. A short
while after the October plenum the decision was taken not to
allow a Party member to hold office in either Party or
government work after he had reached the age of 70.
In principle it was a sensible decision. In 1964 most of the
members of the Presidium and Secretariat of the Central
Committee were under 60. The 82-year-old Otto Kuusinen, a
Finn who had lived in the Soviet Union since 1918 and had been
a member of the Politburo in the 1950s, had died in May of that
year; N. M. Shvernik, aged 76, held the post of chairman of the
Party Commission, not a very demanding job. The only one of
the 'old men' to be affected by the new decision was Mikoyan,
who was 69 in November 1964. Thus at the end of November
1965 Anastas Ivanovich gave notice of his retirement, citing his
age as the reason. The notice was accepted. (It has escaped no

one's notice that the leadership exempted itself from this age rule soon after.)

Mikoyan's work in the Presidium of the Supreme Soviet had not been marked by any especially dramatic incidents, although the case does come to mind of M. P. Yakubovich, his former assistant in the Trade Commissariat, who had been released after twenty-five years of incarceration but not rehabilitated, and who had remained in Karaganda, in the Tikhonov Home for Invalids. His health having somewhat improved, Yakubovich began writing short literary essays, plays on historical themes and sketches of the Bolshevik leaders whom he had met (for instance, L. B. Kamenev, G. E. Zinoviev, Trotsky, Stalin). In 1964 he managed to get to Moscow. At that time I was helping him by typing his notes – it was when *samizdat,* the clandestine circulation of manuscripts, was just starting. On the advice of friends, Yakubovich wrote to Mikoyan asking him to help with his rehabilitation. Many people thought that the new 'All-Union elder statesman' would ignore the hardship of his former assistant, but Mikoyan received him. He told Yakubovich at once that he could do nothing just then to get a political case of 1930–31 reviewed – after all, even the trials of 1936–38 were not yet being reviewed and repealed – but he did telephone D. A. Kunayev, the first secretary of the Central Committee of the Communist Party of Kazakhstan, and asked him to set things to rights for Yakubovich, who, as Mikoyan said, had suffered unjustly during the time of the 'cult'. Yakubovich did not ask to be allowed to move to Moscow but contented himself with a separate room in the Invalid's Home and a pension of 120 roubles a month, which enabled him to do more work and to travel to Moscow more often.

Mikoyan relinquished the post of head of Government at a ceremony attended by much pomp and circumstance. There were speeches of thanks; he was awarded his sixth Order of Lenin. He remained a deputy to the Supreme Soviet from a district in Armenia and a member of the Presidium of the Supreme Soviet. At the Twenty-Third Party Congress in 1966 and at the Twenty-Fourth in 1971 he was elected a member of the Party Central Committee, but he was never again a member of the Politburo.

In the last years of his life Mikoyan devoted less and less attention to state affairs. He did not seek meetings with Brezhnev or Kosygin, nor did he once pay a visit to Khrushchev. In 1967 he expressed interest in the fate of A. M. Nekrich, the Soviet historian who had been expelled from the Party after the publication in 1965 of his book *22 June 1941,* which the Soviet censor had passed. Mikoyan asked friends to acquire a copy of the book for him and also some of the materials on Nekrich's case. He expressed surprise that Nekrich should have been expelled from the Party, but he did not involve himself in the matter any further.

Despite the fact that he had left power without conflict and that he was still a member of the Central Committee and of the Presidium of the Supreme Soviet, Mikoyan was nevertheless suddenly deprived of certain of his privileges. Several times the number of his servants and staff was reduced, but what was especially painful for him was the order to move out of his state dacha near Moscow. It was a big house, practically a manor, that had belonged before the Revolution to a rich Caucasian merchant, and Mikoyan had lived there with his family for nearly half his lifetime.

One of the changes made under Khrushchev had been that all responsible Central Committee workers were thenceforth to be 'emancipated' – that is, at liberty to register themselves as Party members in any one of the 414,000 primary Party organizations throughout the entire system. Mikoyan registered at the Red Proletarian Factory. As he had always done, in retirement he continued to attend Party meetings and conferences at this factory, and sometimes he made speeches and answered queries. Often he accepted invitations from other organizations to talk about his experiences.

On one occasion, in either 1969 or 1970, I was invited to a meeting at the scientific institute run by P. L. Kapitsa, where Mikoyan was going to speak. The auditorium was filled to overflowing, but the welcome accorded to Mikoyan was rather cool, as many people regarded him first and foremost as one of Stalin's right-hand men. Only one person in the hall suddenly jumped up and started clapping; nobody else followed his example. Mikoyan was not troubled by this. From his place in the auditorium, and without notes of any kind, he spoke about several interesting episodes from the 1920s, and then gave us a good few examples of Stalin's senseless, savage acts of terror against scientists and technologists, which Mikoyan naturally condemned.

The audience listened with growing interest. After speaking for a while about some of the problems of trade and supply during the 1930s and the war years, Mikoyan switched, with no apparent dislocation, to the topic of the Cuban missile crisis, and we all heard for the first time about the important role that he had played in averting a fearful war, and about how close the USSR and the USA had come to the brink of disaster. He ended with a description of the funeral of President Kennedy, which had been attended by nearly all the important leaders of the Western world, after which he himself had represented the USSR in unofficial talks in Washington with a number of those leaders. When he had finished reminiscing he dealt deftly and wittily with many questions, some of them extremely pointed, and as the chairman brought the evening to a close, the audience rose and gave Mikoyan a standing ovation.

From 1975 onwards Mikoyan no longer took part in the work of the Supreme Soviet, and he virtually stopped speaking anywhere. He was not present at the Twenty-Fifth Party Congress in 1976, and he was not elected to the new Central Committee. He lived the life of a pensioner, passing the time in the company of the few of his friends who were still alive and the many members of his family.

In the mid-1960s he had started to write his memoirs, fragments of which were published in the journal *Yunost* (*Youth*). Then books began to appear: *Thoughts and Recollections of Lenin* (1970), *By the Path of Struggle* (1971), *The Early 1920s* (1974). A book called *Years, Events, Meetings* was written, prepared for press and even anounced in the publication plans for 1978, but it never saw the light of day. It was removed from the schedules immediately after the news of Mikoyan's death was released.

From what we can read of his works we see that Mikoyan had an extraordinarily accurate memory, but he recorded his recollections only up to the mid-1920s, and we learn nothing

about events between 1926 and 1965. He tells his readers about
trivial differences that arose in the Nizhny-Novgorod provincial Party committee in 1921–22 but nothing about what went
on in the Politburo at the end of the 1920s, let alone in the 1930s
and 1940s. To the very end of his life he retained his
characteristic discretion. Perhaps he wrote something for
himself, with no thought of publishing it? It is not likely. 'What
a story we'd have if Anastas Mikoyan gave us his true
recollections!' the American historian Adam Ulam exclaims in
his book on Stalin, adding that after Mikoyan's death 'we can
be sure that his grief-stricken colleagues will thoroughly and
nervously scrutinize each scrap of paper he leaves behind.'[13]

It will be a long time before we know – if ever. In mid-
October 1978 he developed acute inflammation of the lungs.
Nothing could save him: he died on 21 October. As soon as
Anastas Ivanovich was dead officials of the Marxism–Leninism
Institute presented themselves at his apartment with a special
warrant; after looking over his archives, they took everything
away. A specialist from the MVD was brought in to open the
safe in his study, and all its contents were also removed. Even
his closest relations were not told what his papers contained.[14]

The arrangements for burying people of Mikoyan's standing
are not left to their relations in the Soviet Union. The
announcement of his death that appeared in the papers on
22 October said nothing about the time and place of the funeral.
The brevity of the announcement and the phrase about the
death of 'the veteran member of the Communist Party of the
Soviet Union, the pensioner Mikoyan, A. I.' suggested that
the funeral would be like that of Khrushchev: the coffin containing the body would be transferred immediately from the
morgue to the Novo-Devichy Cemetery. Even Mikoyan's
family did not know if there was to be a lying-in-state. The
decision about the funeral was taken only on 23 October, and
the obituary signed by all the Politburo did not appear in *Pravda*
and other papers until 24 October; but still there was no
mention about a lying-in-state, which prompted his friends to
talk about a 'semi-secret funeral'. In fact, the lying-in-state took
place on 25 October, in Scientists' Club on Kropotkin Street.
Access to the coffin was restricted, and the time for farewells

was limited to no more than a few hours. The mourners were in the main especially selected delegations from a number of Moscow factories and institutions. 'Unorganized' citizens were not allowed into the building. Representatives from Armenia, headed by the republic's leaders, flew in and formed a guard of honour for their countryman.

The young Mikoyan had buried Lenin, accompanying the coffin from Gorki (a village not far from Moscow – now Gorki-Leninskoye) and standing on the tribune that had been hastily knocked together on Red Square. Mikoyan had buried Stalin: he had carried the coffin containing the body out of Unions' House. When Khrushchev died, on his grave were laid wreaths labelled 'From the Mikoyan family' and 'To a dear friend from A. I. Mikoyan'. And now Mikoyan himself was being buried. The guard of honour next to the coffin was made up in turn of Ministers and members of the Presidium of the Supreme Soviet, and during the day Politburo members – L. I. Brezhnev, V. V. Grishin, A. P. Kirilenko, A. N. Kosygin, M. A. Suslov, D. F. Ustinov and B. N. Ponomarev – paid their respects.

I shall not rehearse the speeches that were made at Scientists' Club and at the funeral that took place the same day. Mikoyan's political longevity was not due solely to good luck or cunning, to his flexibility or his capacity to give way to force or make compromises, to his phenomenal diplomatic talents. It was, rather, the consequence of his exceptional efficiency. Even Stalin knew the value of that, for after all many a revolution had occurred because of poor supplies – and not only in Russia.

Mikoyan had looked death in the face more than once. He might have been buried in Baku in 1920, together with his friends of the Baku commune. He could have been shot in 1937, like so many other members of the Party Central Committee and People's Commissars. His remains might have been buried in Red Square, alongside Lenin's Mausoleum, instead of in their final resting place, next to that of his wife, Ashkhen, in the Novo-Devichy Cemetery.

3

M. A. Suslov: 'Ideologist-in-Chief'

At the end of January 1982 the Soviet press and radio announced: 'In his eightieth year, after a prolonged illness, Politburo Member, Secretary of the Party Central Committee, Deputy of the Supreme Soviet, twice a Hero of Socialist Labour, Mikhail Andreyevich Suslov has died.' He was buried four days later with official honours of the kind that no other Party or state leader had been accorded since the funeral of Stalin.

Yet to us Suslov had not seemed like any of the other Soviet political leaders who had attracted the attention of the outside world over the previous fifteen years. Not much had been said or written about him, and he himself had never sought publicity, preferring to remain in the background. He did not chase after prominent state posts; he was never a Minister or deputy chairman of the Council of Ministers; and in the Supreme Soviet he occupied only the modest post of chairman of the Commission on Foreign Affairs. Most of his life was spent working in the Party machine. Like Malenkov, he was above all an *apparatchik,* if a more skilful one. He ascended the rungs of the Party ladder more slowly than many. At the age of 33 both Molotov and Kaganovich, for example, were already Central Committee secretaries. At the same age Mikoyan was even a People's Commissar and a candidate member of the Politburo, and Malenkov was running one of the most important departments of the Central Committee machine. Suslov at 33 was nothing more than a run-of-the-mill inspector in the Party Central Control Commission, yet at the end of his life he was no modest pensioner with honorary membership of the

Central Committee – on the contrary, he was still invested with enormous power and held second place in the Party hierarchy. That is why his death provoked so much comment and speculation.

During his last seventeen years Suslov was considered the Party's chief ideologist. Ideology in the Soviet Union is not merely an aspect of propaganda and agitation or a topic of social science; it is also a vitally important instrument of power. No one can hold an important post in any social or state organization if he does not adhere to the Party ideology of Marxism-Leninism. The foundations of Marxism–Leninism are taught in all schools and institutions of further education, regardless of their type. No higher degree, be it in physics, mathematics, astronomy, literature or law, is awarded before the candidate has sat a preliminary examination in Marxist philosophy. Until recently, anyone accused of departing from Marxist ideology, let alone of disputing its tenets, put more than his career at risk.

As the Politburo member responsible for ideological issues, Suslov stood at the apex of a pyramid of institutions. In the Central Committee he supervised the sections dealing with culture, agitation and propaganda, science, schools and institutions of higher education, two international sections, the political administration of the Soviet Army, the Central Committee's information department and its training commission, and the department dealing with the Komsomol (the Young Communist League) and social organizations. He also had overall control of, and supervised, the Ministry of Culture, the State Publishing Committee, the Cinematography Committee, television and radio, the entire press and censorship apparatus, the official news agency TASS, the Communist Party of the Soviet Union's links with other Communist Parties, and Soviet foreign policy. Naturally, he had to work closely with the KGB and the State Prosecutor's office, particularly when questions arose in connection with the rather obscure notion of 'ideological sabotage'. In this context he encountered considerable difficulties over the 'dissident' movement that developed in the 1960s and 1970s and devoted a great deal of attention to actual control – it is usually termed 'Party' control – of the Writers'

Union, in the most important meetings of which he took part himself. He also controlled the Artists' Union, the Architects' Union, the journalists and cinematograph staff, as well as all the theatres and music-halls, unions of friendship with foreign countries and similar organizations. He ran the system of Party education and the *Znanie* (Knowledge) Society, which provides nationwide lectures on philosophy, Party history and popular science. He was in charge of the publication of school text-books, all social science institutes and state relations with the various religious bodies and church organizations. And even that is not a complete inventory of his responsibilities.

One of his jobs was to organize countless jubilees, such as the fiftieth and then the sixtieth anniversary of Soviet power, the fiftieth anniversary of the formation of the Soviet Union, the centenary of Lenin's birth and a similar celebration ten years later, to mention only a few. He was one of the organizers of the lavish celebration of Stalin's seventieth birthday in 1949, Khrushchev's in 1964 and Brezhnev's in 1976 and of the latter's seventy-fifth in 1981.

Suslov himself was modest in his personal and social life, but he was very good at indulging the vanity of others if need be. On the other hand, many of the jubilee campaigns that he organized were designed to appeal to such primitive instincts and were accompanied by such crude flattery and adulation that many people were compelled to wonder whether he was aiming to exalt or discredit the Party leaders in question.

No one, it seems, would ever have accused Suslov of harbouring a yearning for material or less tangible rewards, of acquisitiveness or of a taste for the extravagances that the possession of power placed within reach. People in the top circles of Soviet society sometimes mocked his asceticism. He was not at all austere, however, when it came to reconciling himself to the weaknesses of his comrades, as long as ideology was not involved. He was frequently extremely indulgent towards prominent Party and state officials who had become involved in corruption or embezzlement. Many a document or report that ought to have prompted an immediate criminal investigation and severe penalties for Ministers, obkom secretaries or heads of entire republics found their final resting place in one of the many safes in Suslov's Kremlin office. That may have been the source of his influence and power.

Solzhenitsyn offers the following portrait of Suslov in his book *The Oak and the Calf:*

> When Tvardovsky [the editor of the journal *Novy Mir*] introduced me to Khrushchev at the Kremlin meeting in December 1962, there was no other member of the Politburo near us and none of them came over. But during the next intermission, when Tvardovsky took me around the foyer and introduced me to such writers, film-makers and artists as he chose, a tall, lean man with an elongated, by no means stupid face came up to us in the cinema annex, took me firmly by the hand and shook it vigorously as he told me how very much he had enjoyed *Ivan Denisovich,* shook it as though from now on I would never have a closer friend. All the others had told me their names, but he did not. I inquired, 'Whom have I the honour to . . .?' and even then the stranger did not declare himself, but Tvardovsky said in a reproachful whisper, 'Mikhail Andreyevich.' I shrugged as much as to say, 'What Mikhail Andreyevich?' 'Su-u-uslov, who else!' said Tvardovsky, doubly reproachful. . . . I just didn't recognize him. Nor indeed did Suslov seem to mind my failure to do so. But here was the puzzle: why had he greeted me so warmly? Khrushchev was nowhere near at the time, and no other Politburo member could see him, so it wasn't to ingratiate himself with anybody. What was it, then? An expression of genuine feeling? To show that there was one vacuum-packed, garden-fresh freedom-lover in the Politburo? The chief ideologist of the Party, no less . . .! Could it be?[1]

The friendliness and modesty that so amazed Solzhenitsyn was in fact only Suslov's customary politeness, which at times might have seemed like obsequiousness if he had been less powerful and less highly placed. He was always extremely courteous to anyone he had invited to his office – to the novelist Vasili Grossman, for instance, who went to see him in 1960. (The topic on that occasion, however, was not to praise but to prohibit Grossman's new novel, *Life and Fate.*)

While many of our leaders have often been distinguished for treating their subordinates with rudeness and contempt, Suslov was almost invariably kind and considerate to even the most humble employee in the Party apparatus, and he was undoubtedly regarded with respect and warmth in many departments.

On the other hand, certain more perceptive observers have reported that the look in Suslov's pale, almost white eyes was unfriendly, and that he was not easy to approach informally. His long, thin fingers were more like those of a pianist than of the peasant that he was by origin. For all his politeness and respect, there were times when he could not hide his coldness and indifference to the fate of others.

One of the chief slogans to emerge from the Central Committee plenum of October 1964 was 'stability' (meaning stability in policies, leadership and ideology); yet the 1960s and 1970s were a time of great change in internal and foreign policy and in the composition of the leadership. By 1981 there remained only three members of the Politburo who had also been members of the then Presidium of the Central Committee when it debated Khrushchev's dismissal in October 1964: L. I. Brezhnev, A. P. Kirilenko and M. A. Suslov. The majority of the others had been removed and the minority buried alongside the Kremlin wall, where they have recently been joined by the earthly remains of Suslov.

Practically nothing is known of the first thirty years of Suslov's life. Entries in the *Great Soviet Encyclopaedia* and the *Historical Encyclopaedia* and the official obituaries all provide the same information, and very sparse it is.

Mikhail Andreyevich Suslov was born on 21 November 1902 in the village of Shakhovskoye, Khvalynsk district, Saratov Province, into the family of an impoverished peasant. His father died many years ago, but his mother lived into her nineties and died in Moscow only at the beginning of the 1970s. I have been unable to discover if there were any other children or, if so, what became of them. At any event, unlike members of the Kaganovich clan, no other Suslovs have played any part in the political life of the country.

Suslov acquired only the most rudimentary elementary education in the village, but he was soon involved in revolutionary activity. By the age of 16 he was already in the

Komsomol and had become a prominent member of the local organization. When the *Kombedy* (committees of poor peasants) were set up in the spring of 1918, Suslov joined the one that was formed at Shakhovskoye, and in 1921 he became a member of the Communist Party.

He was soon sent by the local Party organization to Moscow, where he enrolled at the Prechistensky *rabfak* (workers' faculty), at which he successfully completed the course in 1924. He decided to continue with his studies and entered the Plekhanov Institute of Agriculture in Moscow; having completed that course with success too, he went on to gain higher qualifications at the Red Professors' Economics Institute, which trained 'Red' teachers to become the new Party intelligentsia. The teaching staff at the Institute was excellent, and it may be taken for granted that Suslov received a sound training in economics. Internal Party debate in the 1920s centred in general on questions of economics and political economy and, more concretely, on the economics of the transitional period. From what we know of Suslov's past, it seems that he fought equally hard against both the 'right opposition' and the 'left'.

Soon the young 'Red' professor was himself teaching political economy at Moscow University and at the Industrial Academy, where, as it happened, N. S. Khrushchev was a student in 1929–30. Relations between the teachers and their students, who had come to the Academy from active Party work, were quite different in those days from what they are today; moreover, as Khrushchev had been elected secretary of the Party organization at the Academy, one may safely assume that he and Suslov knew each other at that time, though nothing that could be called friendship apparently existed between them. That only occurred at the end of the 1940s.

In 1931 Suslov was offered a job in the Party apparatus and gave up teaching. He became an inspector in the Party Central Control Commission and the People's Commissariat for Workers' and Peasants' Inspection. His primary task in this post was to sort out countless 'personal cases' – that is, infringements of Party discipline and the Party Statutes, and appeals by people who had been expelled. Apparently, he was quite good at it.

In 1933–34 he headed a commission to purge the Party in the Urals and Chernigov oblasts, as part of the Union-wide purge that was being supervised by Kaganovich, who would undoubtedly have noticed this particularly diligent member of his commission. Many people are convinced that Suslov was responsible for the repressions that took place in Rostov (the town and the province), but their assumption is based only on the fact that Suslov happened to be engaged in important Party work there during the years of the terror. Suslov himself said several times to friends that far from destroying it, he rebuilt the Rostov Party organization. That is as maybe. The fact is, we have no evidence of his personal involvement in the repressive campaigns of 1937–38, though they certainly paved the way for his rapid rise. Thus, in 1937, when practically the entire leadership of the Rostov provincial Party committee was liquidated, he was sent there to manage affairs. The savage repressions continued, but they did not touch Suslov, who soon became obkom secretary.

Arrests in the province were so widespread that some enterprises were entirely without Party organizers, and the Party organization in general was bleeding to death. Thousands of non-Party engineers and economic managers were also arrested, their places often being taken by ordinary workers or 'Stakhanovites', who could hardly stand in for practised experts and ensure the fulfilment of the quotas. One such 'Stakhanovite' was N. A. Izotov, who ran the coal mining in the province and who on one occasion, in a fury, struck the boss of the local NKVD who had come to request his sanction for some new arrests. The outcome was the dismissal not of Izotov but of the NKVD official. Beria was People's Commissar for Internal Affairs at the time, and V. S. Abakumov was sent to Rostov to run the NKVD there. A number of prisoners were released and given back their former jobs; the provincial Party committee reviewed appeals by Party members who had been expelled from the Party but not arrested; and before the Eighteenth Party Congress Suslov organized the rapid intake of 3,000 new members.

The Party organization of the vast Stavropol kray (territory) was also bled white by the repressions, and in 1939 Suslov was sent there as first obkom secretary, a major step in his career. It was from Stavropol that he took part in the work of the Eighteenth Party Congress, at which, although he did not speak, he was appointed a member of the Central Revision Commission. Two years later, at the Eighteenth Party Conference, he became a member of the Central Committee: another important stage in his Party career was complete.

The war reached Stavropol in 1942. As the Germans developed their summer offensive, they seized Rostov-on-Don and began rapidly to advance through the Northern Caucasus. The Red Army's retreat was so fast and so disorderly that in some areas of the territory units moved east several days before any German divisions arrived. It proved possible to halt the German advance only near the town of Ordzhonikidze, a few days' march from Grozny. The German occupation, however, lasted less than a year, and during that time Suslov's chief task as obkom secretary was to organize the partisan movement. He ran the headquarters of the Stavropol partisan detachments, and, while fighting was still in progress in the Northern Caucasus, he also became a member of the War Council of the Northern Group, Transcaucasian Front.

During the war and the enemy occupation a small section of the Karachay population of Stavropol supported the German administration, and a 'Karachay National Committee' was set up in the town of Mikoyan-Shakhar. Most of the Karachays, however, supported the partisan movement and not the Committee. Nevertheless, in November 1943, as soon as the area had been liberated, the whole Karachay population, numbering some 70,000, was deported from its native land and dispatched by the trainload to 'special settlements' in Central Asia and Kazakhstan; the Karachay–Circassian Autonomous Oblast was liquidated. Obviously, the decision to deport the Muslim nationalities from the Northern Caucasus and the Volga region was taken in Moscow by the State Defence Committee, but it is equally certain that the Stavropol Party committee gave its full support to this decision and helped to implement it.

During operations in the Northern Caucasus one of those who came under Suslov as a member of the War Council was

Colonel L. I. Brezhnev, who was at that time head of the Political Section of the Eighteenth Army, and it was Brezhnev in particular who helped Suslov to revive the civilian and economic life of the area. Theirs was a brief acquaintance, however, as the Eighteenth Army moved west after the taking of Novorossiisk.

It is worth pointing out in this connection that ten years later Brezhnev, by then a lieutenant-general, was appointed deputy head of the Chief Political Administration of the Soviet Army and Navy, and during this period he again had to carry out the directives of Central Committee Secretary M. A. Suslov. Certain books on Soviet history suggest that at that time something like a political alliance had already developed between Brezhnev and the older and more highly placed Suslov. One author even hints that Suslov, foreseeing an inevitable confrontation with Khrushchev, who was emerging as the front-runner, began to promote Brezhnev as a future successor.[2] This proposition is untenable, for during the period 1953–54 both Suslov and Brezhnev offered Khrushchev unswerving loyalty. But let us return to Suslov's career.

At the end of 1944 he was given a new appointment as chairman of the Central Committee's bureau for Lithuanian affairs. Lithuania had recently been liberated from German occupation, but the situation there was extremely complex. A considerable proportion of the population was opposed to 'sovietization', and after the Germans had left, stubborn resistance to the new authority developed into a prolonged and bitter civil war, in which one part of the local population supported the Red Army, while the other was engaged in armed opposition to it. The partisan units of 'forest brethren' were a mixed bunch and included not only people who had collaborated with the German occupying forces, rich peasants and children of the Lithuanian bourgeoisie but also simple folk who were fighting for the freedom of their country. It was a hard and bloody struggle, in the course of which a substantial part of the republic's population was quite simply deported to Siberia. Representatives of the bourgeoisie and other 'alien' classes, members of the former Lithuanian administration and leaders of the national political parties were removed from the cities, while peasants suspected of giving help to the 'forest brethren' were expelled from the rural districts. It took two years of military operations to destroy the partisan movement in the republic completely. The struggle, which was accompanied by savagery and widespread violence on both sides, left an indelible mark on the minds of the Lithuanian people.

Stalin's emissary in Lithuania was Suslov, who was invested with such extraordinary powers that his influence spread into the neighbouring Baltic republics as well. Not surprisingly, he was not well loved in that region, and when he died there were many in Lithuania and the other Baltic republics who could not conceal their delight.

Suslov went to Lithuania, as to the front, without his family, which continued to live in more peaceful Stavropol. After the death of I. D. Chernyakhovsky, a young and talented general who had commanded one of the Baltic fronts, Suslov took his widow under his own care and was soon so infatuated with the beautiful young woman that he virtually abandoned his own family. His wife appealed to Stalin, but the leader was utterly indifferent to the countless cases of infidelity among his comrades-in-arms, and anyway he seems to have regarded women with the deepest contempt. He did not encourage divorce, however; Suslov was given a stern reprimand, and he returned to his family.

Stalin was evidently completely satisfied with Suslov's work, and in 1947 Suslov was transferred to Moscow and made a Central Committee secretary. (The Secretariat at that time consisted of A. A. Zhdanov, A. A. Kuznetsov, G. M. Malenkov, G. M. Popov and Stalin himself.) In the same year he replaced G. F. Aleksandrov as head of the Central Committee department of agitation and propaganda. He took part in the campaign against the 'rootless cosmopolitans', and in 1948 he had headed a commission to investigate the activities of Yu. A. Zhdanov, the head of a scientific department who had dared to criticize the spurious theories of the biologist Lysenko. Enjoying Stalin's complete confidence, in January 1948 Suslov was deputed by the Central Committee to read the speech at its remembrance ceremony on the twenty-fourth anniversary of

Lenin's death. As chief editor of *Pravda* (1949–50) and as a member of the Presidium of the Supreme Soviet, in 1949 he represented the Central Committee at the Budapest Conference of the Communist Parties' Information Bureau (Cominform) and gave a speech devoted chiefly to condemning the Yugoslav Communist Party. Nevertheless, his role as an ideologist in those years was restricted, for the chief 'ideologist' and 'theoretician' in the Party was still Stalin himself.

A few years later, speaking at the Twentieth Party Congress, Suslov described the abnormal situation that had existed in the field of ideology under Stalin:

> There is no doubt that the spread of mindless dogmatism was greatly enhanced by the cult of personality, whose worshippers ascribed the development of Marxist theory to certain individuals and pinned their hopes entirely on them. All other mortals, supposedly, had only to absorb and popularize what those individuals created. Thus the role of the collective mind of our Party and of the fraternal Parties, and of the collective experience of the popular masses, was ignored.[3]

We can be quite certain, however, that once he had become the Party's chief ideologist Suslov, who had been raised in and moulded by the Stalinist period, was himself stamped with dogmatism, and that the fear of independence and originality remained with him throughout his life. From the time of his very first appearances in the ideological arena onwards, his primary object was to commit no ideological error – that is to say, never to come into conflict with the political aims of the ruling hierarchy. He understood perfectly well that mediocrity and monotony in an ideological speech would make him a target for no one, whereas the least deviation from doctrinal orthodoxy would signal the end of his entire political career.

At the Nineteenth Party Congress Stalin included Suslov in the enlarged (and renamed) Central Committee Presidium, an appointment that indicated great trust, as it introduced Suslov at last into Stalin's immediate circle – and into an area of considerable hidden dangers. In December 1952 Stalin, who was for some reason dissatisfied with him, said sharply, 'If you don't want to work, you can leave your job.' Suslov replied that he would work wherever the Party wanted him to. 'We shall see,' Stalin replied, with a hint of a threat, but the incident did not develop into a full-scale confrontation.

Suslov remained in the Presidium for only a few months; soon after Stalin's death, when the Presidium was reduced in size, he was no longer a member of it, though he did remain a Central Committee secretary.

Khrushchev was the polar opposite of Suslov in character. Extraordinarily energetic, prone to making changes and initiating reforms, he could not stand any kind of dogmatism, quite unlike the cautious and secretive Suslov. In his administration Khrushchev was his own chief ideologist and Foreign Minister, and he maintained direct relations with the leaders of other Communist Parties himself. What he needed, however, was a member of the Presidium who would see to the everyday running of the countless ideological institutions. His eye fell upon Suslov, who became a member of the Presidium in 1955.

Khrushchev can hardly have found Suslov's activity very much to his liking, but since the early 1950s Suslov's relations with Malenkov had been very cool, and Suslov knew that if Malenkov should come out on top, things would not go well for him or for those whom he protected. It is not surprising therefore that in the bitter struggle that soon developed between Khrushchev and the so-called 'anti-Party group', Suslov gave Khrushchev staunch backing. At the Twentieth Party Congress he voiced his support for Khrushchev's views, and at the turbulent Presidium meeting of June 1957, which was crucial for Khrushchev, Suslov opened with a speech outlining the main sources of disagreement and again making clear his support for Khrushchev. After him came Molotov, Malenkov, Kaganovich and Bulganin, who repeated their charges against Khrushchev. Fearful that defeat would threaten more than just their careers, they put up a stiff defence of their positions, and the plenum therefore lasted several days, during which time Suslov never wavered.

In the late 1950s and early 1960s, however, Suslov himself started cautiously to oppose many aspects of Khrushchev's foreign and domestic policies. He was against further exposure of Stalin. He insisted that the question of the 'anti-Party group' not be raised at the Twenty-First or Twenty-Second Party Congresses, but Khrushchev acted on his own initiative in this matter; and as far as ideological counsel was concerned, he settled many questions with the help of L. F. Ilyichov or Mikoyan and consulted no 'ideologist-in-chief'.

In the first phase of the dispute with China, when the polemics were still of an ideological character, Suslov acted as the chief opponent to Liu Shao-chi, Deng Hsiao-ping and even Mao Tse-tung, and he was responsible for editing all the correspondence from the Chinese Party Central Committee. In February 1964 he gave the chief report on the Sino–Soviet dispute at the Central Committee Plenum. In 1956, together with Mikoyan and Zhukov, he had gone to Hungary in order to supervise the suppression of the uprising in Budapest, and in 1962 he was sent, again with Mikoyan, to Novocherkassk to suppress strikes and demonstrations that had been provoked by an increase in the price of meat and dairy products and by the shortage of food. Mikoyan told friends later that he had been in favour of holding talks with workers' representatives but that Suslov had insisted on the suppression of the unrest by force. Suslov took an active part in that same year in helping to draft the new Party Programme.

When explaining the outcome of the June plenum or the Twenty-Second Congress, Suslov frequently exclaimed, 'We will not allow our dear Nikita Sergeyevich [Khrushchev] to be insulted!' Yet in the spring of 1964, if not earlier, it was Suslov himself who initiated confidential discussions with members of the Central Committee Presidium, and with a number of influential members of the Central Committee, about the issue of Khrushchev's removal from the leadership. His main allies were A. N. Shelepin, who had recently become head of the Party/State Control Committee, having moved from being head of the KGB only in 1961, and N. G. Ignatov, who had lost his post in the Presidium following the Twenty-Second Congress but was still head of the Central Committee Bureau for the RSFSR. The chairman of the KGB, V. E. Semichastny, also had a hand in organizing and running the October 1964 plenum of the Central Committee, and all of them were involved in the decision to remove Khrushchev from office, while it was Suslov who reported to the plenum on all of Khrushchev's transgressions and mistakes. From both the political and the theoretical point of view his speech was a wretched one, utterly devoid of any attempt at an analysis of the situation that had developed.

After Khrushchev's enforced retirement, the Party leaders proclaimed – not for the first time – the need for 'collective leadership' and the inadmissibility of any new 'cult of personality'. Although Brezhnev had become First (and from 1966 General) Secretary of the Party, he did not yet wield as much power as he would in the 1970s. Almost as much influence had accrued, through the Party/state apparatus, to Suslov and Shelepin, who were jockeying behind the scenes for position in the Party hierarchy. By the end of 1965 it looked as if 'Iron Shurik' (Shelepin) had gained the upper hand, and many of his friends were congratulating themselves on the fact that he would be the next First Secretary. Thanks to his greater experience, however, Suslov managed to squeeze Shelepin out, and he became not First but 'Third' secretary of the Central Committee. Suslov also succeeded in arranging for the dismissal of Ilyichov from the Secretariat and his replacement by P. N. Demichev, who, as a specialist in chemical engineering, might have coped perfectly well as first secretary of the Moscow city Party committee but as the Central Committee secretary for ideology was weak, incompetent and lacking in initiative. The more observant delegates at the Twenty-Third Party Congress in spring of 1966 noticed that it was Suslov who stage-managed the meeting.

One of Suslov's enemies in the Central Committee turned out to be C. P. Trapeznikov, a protégé of Brezhnev, who headed the section on science, schools and institutes of higher education. Apart from running this important section of the Central Committee, Trapeznikov also led the campaign for the rehabilitation of Stalin, which gathered force in 1965–66. Suslov considered this policy unwise, or at any rate premature, and he therefore tried to restrain the impulse of Trapeznikov and his supporters. In 1966 five academic historians, including A. M. Nekrich, wrote Suslov a detailed and reasoned protest against attempts to rehabilitate Stalin. Suslov's assistant, V. Vorontsov, told them that Suslov agreed with them and that they would hear him give a reply to their letter at the Twenty-Third Party Congress. But neither Suslov nor many other members of the Politburo spoke at the Congress, and when the Party Control Commission was discussing Nekrich's expulsion from the Party in 1967, Suslov declined to give him a personal interview and refused to interfere in the Control Commission's business.

Another victory for the Stalinists over the more moderate elements in the leadership was also seen in the removal of *Pravda*'s chief editor, A. M. Rumyantsev, around whom a group of talented writers and journalists had earlier formed. Prompted by the defection to the USA of Stalin's daughter, Svetlana Alliluyeva, and the KGB's failed attempts to get her back to the USSR, Suslov insisted on the removal of KGB chairman, V. E. Semichastny, a close friend of Shelepin, and his replacement by Yu. V. Andropov, who had been in charge of one of the Central Committee's international bureaux under Suslov's supervision.

The events that took place in Czechoslovakia in 1967–68 greatly alarmed Suslov, who feared that the same thing might be happening there as had happened in Hungary in 1956. When differences arose in the Politburo, he was staunchly in favour of sending in Warsaw Pact troops.

Suslov did not support the nearly completed plan for Stalin's rehabilitation, which was timed to coincide with the ninetieth anniversary of the former leader's birth; yet at the same time, the end of 1969, he virtually directed the dispersal of the former editorial board of the journal *Novy Mir* (*New World*), which at that time expressed the mood of the most progressive section of the Soviet creative intelligentsia. When the journal's chief editor, A. T. Tvardovsky, finally managed to get through to him on the telephone to voice his protest, Suslov said, 'Calm down, Comrade Tvardovsky. Just do what the Central Committee says.' Frequently an entire edition of a book would be banned from sale; when publishers complained to Suslov about the waste of labour and expense, he would tell them, 'We don't economize on ideology.'

Whether Suslov thought he might one day become the head of the Party we do not know. He was certainly irritated by Brezhnev's growing authority and by the ramifications of his personal power machine, as well as by the independence with which he frequently acted and spoke. At the Central Committee plenum in late 1969 Brezhnev made a speech in which he criticized many shortcomings in economic policy and management. The speech had been prepared by his assistants and consultants and had not been debated in the Politburo beforehand. As Brezhnev was not giving the keynote speech at the plenum and was speaking merely in the normal course of debate, he was not infringing any of the conventions of the 'collective leadership'. Despite that, the speech was taken to be an expression of policy. After the plenum Suslov, Shelepin and K. T. Mazurov, a Politburo member and first deputy chairman of the Council of Ministers, sent a letter to the Central Committee containing a number of critical comments about Brezhnev's speech. It was to be expected that the dispute would come up at the Central Committee's spring plenum, but the meeting never took place, as Brezhnev managed to enlist the support of the Central Committee's most influential members in advance, and Suslov, Shelepin and Mazurov withdrew their criticism. Shelepin continued to raise questions designed to discomfit Brezhnev in an effort to strengthen his own influence in the leadership; for his pains he was first made leader of the trade unions and then removed from the Politburo altogether. Having managed to retain a certain degree of independence, Suslov fell silent and contented himself with second place in the Party hierarchy and the role of 'ideologist-in-chief'.

Suslov and his apparatus controlled the entire ideological life of the country in the 1970s. One could perhaps, if one wished, point to some positive achievements in the fields of science and culture during the decade, but on the whole it was a period of regression, and for that we have to thank Suslov's leadership. The 1960s had witnessed many signs of progress in all branches of culture, art and the social sciences, but most advances had stagnated and begun to fade by the end of the decade, and they were totally extinguished in the 1970s, which were a bad time for intellectuals and anybody else who was in cultural affairs. And as Suslov himself made no special contribution to either Party theory or ideology, his creative potential turned out to be astonishingly limited.

What cannot be disputed is that he was a very good *apparatchik*. He knew his way about the corridors of power; he had extremely good contacts in military circles and in the KGB; and he always maintained friendly relations with representatives of the creative intelligentsia – though by no means the best of them. As I have already noted, he always behaved modestly, even towards the humblest assistants in his apparatus, and he would invariably shake hands with every visitor. His way of life was frugal: he was not given to having luxurious villas built for himself; he did not hold lavish receptions; and he avoided strong drink. He did not take much interest in his children's careers – his daughter, Maya, and his son, Revoly, never held important positions. He himself had no scientific degree or title and sought none, unlike Ilyichov, who was made an Academician, or Trapeznikov, who after several attempts finally attained Corresponding Membership of the Academy of Sciences. On the contrary, Suslov was responsible for introducing in the Central Committee a rule forbidding executives in responsible posts from trying to obtain academic titles. Nevertheless, it is safe to assume that Suslov had a detailed knowledge of Marxism and Leninism – meaning that he knew the basic texts. No doubt all this was laudable: his intellectual capacity and ideological orthodoxy would have equipped him admirably to be a good teacher of the social sciences, but for the chief ideologist of the Communist Party of the Soviet Union they were woefully inadequate.

The obituaries speak of Suslov as the Party's 'great theoretician'; in fact, he added nothing new to Party theory made not one original remark. In his thirty-five years in top jobs in the Central Committee he did not write a single book, and nearly all his works fit into two medium-sized volumes. And what works they are! They are impossibly boring to read straight through, and he uses the same expressions and ideological

clichés in one speech after another, in one article after another.
It is as if he were consciously avoiding bright new thoughts and
telling comparisons. Moreover, he never makes a joke, and his
speeches are never punctuated by asides like 'laughter', 'loud
laughter', 'stirring in the hall' and so on. Oddly enough, one of
his chief assistants, Vorontsov, was a great collector of sayings
and aphorisms, yet when he was preparing Suslov's speeches he
was never allowed to include anything of interest from his
collection; and in general Suslov's speech writers remark that he
very rarely made any alterations, except to delete a phrase or
two or the occasional paragraph. What, then, is to be found in
his works, which were published in 1977, and in a supplementary booklet that came out in 1980?

The speeches that he made as secretary of the Rostov and
Stavropol provincial Party committees, like the speeches of any
similar functionary, deal with the usual issues: the task of the
Komsomol in training the young, the job of the village teacher
in bringing the light of learning to the people, the importance of
the timely and proper working of the land, the need to work
conscientiously for the front and to fight bravely in the war. As
a responsible Central Committee executive, Suslov said
nothing more profound or more significant. A good fifth of all
his speeches were made on occasions when decorations were
being bestowed on numerous towns and oblasts, and they were
doubtless written on his behalf by someone in the Central
Committee of the relevant obkom apparatus, just as they would
have been drafted for anyone else who was obliged to make
speeches on such occasions.

Suslov gave these ready-made speeches at countless congresses of foreign Communist Parties, but even the speeches
that he traditionally made as a Politburo member at election
meetings, in the various districts that returned him as a deputy
to the Supreme Soviet, were entirely lacking in any originality.
A large part of his 'cultural legacy' comprises anniversary
speeches: those given to mark Lenin's birthday, the October
Revolution, the Second Party Congress, the Seventh Comintern Congress, Karl Marx's 150th birthday, fifty years of the
Soviet Union and so on. On occasions when Brezhnev gave an
anniversary speech Suslov would have a similar one published

in the journal *Kommunist*. The regular lectures he gave at All-Union gatherings of ideological workers or social science teachers are not very interesting either. As a rule, he tried to avoid difficult or topical questions, and he would carefully edit his speeches and articles for reprinting, deleting praise or censure of either Stalin or Khrushchev and any examples of Molotov's misdeeds.

It is hardly surprising, therefore, that there has never been much demand for his collected speeches and articles in the bookshops. It took two years to sell the first edition of 100,000 copies, though the books were to be found on every bookstall. This is not a large print run by Soviet standards, especially as there are at least 1 million people who are professionally engaged in ideological work and the social sciences. Thus one may assume that the second impression, which was also to run to 100,000 copies, was never printed. A supplementary collection of his speeches and articles for 1977–80, priced at only 30 kopeks, was printed – the print run was 50,000 copies, a derisory quantity for any political booklet – but stock of this work was cleared only because copies were distributed to libraries and Party offices. Perhaps no more than 20,000 or 30,000 teachers and propagandists forked out the 2 roubles in order to add the three volumes of Suslov's works to their private collections. Not a very encouraging end to the long career of the Party's 'ideologist-in-chief'.

Mikhail Suslov was not very strong physically. As a child he contracted tuberculosis, and later in life he developed diabetes. After stormy scenes with his assistants in Stavropol or Lithuania he was subject to convulsions similar to epileptic fits. He had a heart attack in 1976, after which he obeyed his doctor's orders and cut down his work to three or four hours a day.

While most government cars travel with their escorting vehicles in reserved lanes at speeds of up to 75 m.p.h., Suslov never allowed his driver to exceed 40. He occasionally used to stop the car at the Historical Museum and stroll from the 'Eternal Flame' through the Alexander Garden to the Kremlin, but he could not allow himself to walk any further. If he suffered from chest pains, he would stay overnight in a special ward at the government hospital on Granovsky Street.

Yet he had a hand in all the main decisions affecting the 'dissidents', from Solzhenitsyn's expulsion and Sakharov's exile to the arrest of the Helsinki human rights groups. It was also at this time that he established good relations with the artist Ilya Glazunov, regarded as the chief representative of the 'Russists', members of an unofficial movement of Russian nationalists. Glazunov, who for years had been regarded virtually as an artist in disgrace, was given permission to stage a great exhibition of his own works in the Manège, which is a very high honour indeed for a Soviet artist. This did not signify Suslov's support for the Russian nationalists, however; it reflected rather the fact that Glazunov had painted a portrait of Suslov that he liked very much. Suslov's dogmatism would not allow him to become an ally of the motley group of nationalists, who anyway had other patrons among the leadership. Moreover, it was Suslov who in 1970 organized a special debate in the Politburo at which the journal *Molodaya Gvardiya* (*Young Guard*) was condemned for publishing nationalistic works and its editorial board dismissed.

Suslov was seriously alarmed by the stormy events that took place in Poland from August 1980, and he gave them his undivided attention. He undertook a trip there in the spring of 1981 in an effort to dissuade the Central Committee of the Polish Party from sanctioning an extraordinary Party congress on the basis of freely elected delegates, outside the control of the Party apparatus. He managed only to get the congress postponed, but he was responsible both for the Soviet Central Committee's letter to the Polish Central Committee and for running the cautious but no less insistent struggle against so-called 'Eurocommunism'.

At the beginning of January 1982 a considerable number of urgent and important matters were vying for Suslov's attention. There was martial law in Poland and sharp differences with the Italian Communist Party because of it; Central Committee Secretary M. V. Zimyanin and the Institute of Marxism–Leninism were quarrelling over the Moscow Arts Theatre's production of *Thus Will We Conquer!*, a play by Mikhail Shatrov about Lenin's last years; several cases of embezzlement and corruption were pending in which certain highly placed officials turned out to be involved. Suslov was unaccustomed to so much stress. He was old. He was suffering from hardening of the arteries and had been instructed not to do too much work or to become over-anxious. At his level of responsibility, however, it was impossible for him not to worry; arguments and tension provoked by bad news were inevitable. After one apparently calm conversation, of which the subject matter was nevertheless extremely stressful, his blood pressure rose. He had a sudden brain haemorrhage, lost consciousness and was dead a few days later.

His death aroused much comment and speculation, but few of the people who filed past his coffin in the Hall of Columns in Union House or watched the funeral ceremony on television felt any real grief and sorrow. There are not many plots left in the small cemetery alongside the Kremlin walls, but one was found for Suslov, next to Stalin's.

4

V. M. Molotov: Muscovite Pensioner

A friend of mine was hurrying to work one day when she found she had left her watch at home. Walking along Granovsky Street in Moscow, she noticed a little old man standing on the pavement. 'Have you the time?' she asked him. 'Thank God,' he replied, raising his head, 'I still have time.' My friend's father had been an important Chekist in the 1920s and 1930s, and he had been shot in 1937. Suddenly she realized with amazement that the old man was none other than Molotov, who had headed the Soviet Government for more than ten years before the war and whose name had invariably been listed second only to Stalin's among the members of the Party Central Committee up to the late 1940s.

Molotov's name is still found, though rarely, in some of the more substantial books on the history of the Soviet Union or of the Party. There is even a short entry on him in the latest edition of the *Great Soviet Encyclopedia*. Most of the young people to whom I have talked lately, however, do not have the slightest idea who he is. It does not surprise me, though it did surprise the thoughtful American journalist, Hedrick Smith, who wrote:

> Westerners forget that, far from the scene, they sometimes know more about some Soviet historical events than young Russians themselves. . . . Arkady Raikin, the famous Soviet stage comic . . . had been hospitalized one winter by a heart attack and was being visited by his 18-year-old grandson. . . . Suddenly, Raikin bolted upright in bed, startled at the sight of Stalin's closest living deputy, former Prime Minister and Foreign Minister Vyacheslav Molotov, passing the door of his hospital room.

'There he goes!' gulped Raikin to his grandson.

'Who?' asked the lad, not recognising the figure, banished from the pages of the Soviet press almost throughout the boy's lifetime.

'Molotov,' mumbled Raikin.

'Who is Molotov?' asked the boy in stunning ignorance.[1]

But people of the older generation remember Molotov well enough, though few of them have any idea of the ex-premier's situation or even whether he is still alive.

Molotov is indeed still alive; in March 1982 he reached the age of 92. He joined the Communist Party in 1906, and if he had not been expelled after the Twenty-Second Congress, he would be one of the Party's oldest living members. (The oldest member in recent years was F. R. Knunyants, who joined the Social Democratic movement in 1902; she died in 1980 at the age of 97.) Molotov is the only living member of the Party Central Committee of the early 1920s.

Molotov's real name is Skryabin. His first writings in the Bolshevik press – short notices and articles – appeared under various pseudonyms. It was in 1918, in a pamphlet on the participation of the workers in the building of the economy, that he first adopted 'Molotov' as a *nom de plume,* and that was the name by which he was known ever after.

For some reason it has often been thought that Molotov's family were gentry. This was not the case. He was born on 9 March 1890 in the village of Kukarka, in Vyatka Province, the third son of Mikhail Skryabin, a town-dweller of Nolinsk.[2] His father was well-to-do and saw that his sons received a reasonable education. Vyacheslav went to secondary school in Kazan and even studied music. It was a time of revolution in Russia, and most of the young people in Kazan held very radical views. He joined one of the self-improvement circles where Marxist literature was read and where he formed a friendship with Victor Tikhomirnov, the son of a wealthy merchant and hier to a great fortune, who had nevertheless joined the Bolshevik group in Kazan in 1905. It was under Tikhomirnov's influence that Molotov also joined the Bolsheviks in 1906. In

1907 he was arrested and exiled to Vologda. His exile over, in 1907 he went to Petersburg, where he enrolled at the Polytechnic Institute. At about that time the first legal Bolshevik paper, *Pravda,* began to circulate in the capital; one of its organizers was Tikhomirnov, who donated large sums to cover the paper's needs. Tikhomirnov asked Molotov to join the staff of the paper, in which he published some short articles.

At the outbreak of the First World War the leadership of the Party, both in Petersburg and in the country at large, was gravely depleted as a result of the arrest and exile of many of its chief figures. It was not until the autumn of 1915 that A. S. Shlyapnikov managed to organize the Petersburg Bureau of the Central Committee, and Molotov, now 25, became a member. It was natural therefore that in the early days of the February Revolution of 1917 he should have appeared to be a prominent figure. By March of that year he was a member of the enlarged Central Committee, of the *Pravda* editorial board and of the Executive Committee of the Petrograd Soviet.

Once the Party leadership began to return from exile, however, Molotov was relegated to the second rank. He was no orator; he was not a man of strong will; and he had little revolutionary fervour. He could hardly shine in the stormy months of revolution in 1917, nor during the years of civil war that followed. But he did reveal himself to be efficient, painstaking and diligent. Moreover, he had almost completed his technical education. In 1918 he headed the Northern District Economic Council, which embraced seven former provinces and the Karelian labour commune. In 1919 he organized the reconstruction of the economy and set up the soviet institutions of the Volga region. In the summer of 1919 he got to know N. K. Krupskaya, Lenin's wife, when they were both on a trip on the agitprop train *Red Star.* His acquaintance with Lenin himself had begun earlier, when he presented Lenin with a copy of his pamphlet on workers' participation in socialist construction.

Sharp conflicts with local organizers led to Molotov's recall and redeployment in the Ukraine, however. As was only to be expected with a one-party system, the central apparatus was expanding fast at that time. In March 1919 the death occurred of Ya. M. Sverdlov, who had run the Party apparatus efficiently and virtually single-handedly, and it was decided to create a Central Committee Secretariat on collective lines. At a Central Committee plenum in 1920 N. N. Krestinsky, E. N. Preobrazhensky and L. P. Serebryakov – all of them supporters of Trotsky – were appointed secretaries. After the 'trade union debate', during which the independence of trade unions was discussed, Lenin decided to create a completely new Secretariat, and this aim was finally achieved after the Tenth Party Congress in 1921, at which Trotsky's platform and his entire group suffered defeat. The new Secretariat and the Central Committee now included Molotov. He became not only executive secretary of the Central Committee but also a candidate member of the Politburo. He did not head the Secretariat for long, however. Although he showed extraordinary zeal for office work, he lacked initiative and authority. Moreover, Lenin was extremely irritated by all the bureaucracy that he detested so much and that was so typical of the work of many of the departments spawned by the Party's Central Committee right from the start. Thus in the spring of 1922 the decision was taken to reorganize the Secretariat once again, to broaden its authority and functions and to put it in the charge of a member of the Politburo. G. Ye. Zinoviev, head of the Party in Leningrad and chairman of Comintern, and L. B. Kamenev, the deputy Prime Minister, nominated Stalin for the post, and Lenin agreed.

After the Eleventh Congress in 1924 the Secretariat of the Central Committee was reconstituted under Stalin, Molotov and V. V. Kuybyshev. Having by now become General Secretary, Stalin retained Molotov in the Secretariat, partly because of his unquestioning loyalty but also because he valued Molotov's bureaucratic efficiency and capacity for hard work. He was certainly not leadership material – he was hardly ever to be seen mixing with workers and peasants; on the other hand, he could be relied on to sit in his office and carry out the huge number of clerical jobs that devolved upon the Secretariat and that Stalin did not especially like to do himself. Old-guard Bolsheviks, who did not much care for office efficiency either, had a nickname for Molotov even in those days – they called him 'Stony-Arse'.

During the 1920s Molotov was almost always to be seen at Stalin's side. He played an active part in the struggle against the Trotskyist opposition and, later, against the Zinovievite and the 'united' opposition. At Party congresses it was usually Molotov who gave the reports on organizational matters. He also wrote frequently in *Pravda* and published a succession of pamphlets and books, including *Questions of Party Work, Lenin and the Party during the Revolution, The Lessons of Trotskyism, Party Policy in the Countryside*. Although he had never displayed any expertise where agrarian problems were concerned, he nevertheless headed the Central Committee commission on work in the countryside from 1924 on. In 1928 and 1929, now a full member of the Politburo, he gave unwavering support to Stalin in his fight with the so-called 'right deviation'. When the Moscow Party organization, which was sympathetic to the 'right', was removed, Molotov took over the leadership of the organization, while retaining his job as one of the Central Committee Secretaries.

Cold and efficient, apparently unhampered by any emotion, Molotov carried out any and all of Stalin's decrees and directives without hesitation. And Stalin rewarded his obedience. When A. I. Rykov retired and left vacant the post of Chairman of the Council of Peoples' Commissars (Sovnarkom), Stalin put forward Molotov as the new head of the Soviet government. In December 1930, at a session of the Central Committee and Control Commission of the Party, Molotov made a speech in which he said:

> Now, in view of my new appointment, I cannot refrain from saying a few words about myself and about my work. . . . For me, as a Communist, there is no greater desire than to be a pupil of Lenin in my job – nor could there be. It fell to me to work under Lenin's direct supervision for only a short time. In recent years it has been my lot . . . to attend the school of Bolshevik work under the direct leadership of Comrade Stalin, and I am proud of that. Up to now it has fallen to me to work as a Party worker. I declare to you, comrades, that I enter upon my work

for the Sovnarkom also in the capacity of Party worker, as a conduit for the will of the Party and of its Central Committee.[3]

Although the main burden of building Soviet industry rested on the shoulders of the People's Commissars and their chief assistants, Molotov had a considerable amount of work to do during the time of the first and second Five-Year Plans. He did not get on with everyone: he had frequent arguments with the Peoples' Commissar for Heavy Industry, G. K. Ordzhonikidze, for instance, and with S. S. Lobov and others, but usually he could count on Stalin's support. Stalin valued Molotov's unflagging and loyal labour, but he also liked the fact that Molotov was short. Anyone who was tall, strong or good-looking irritated the stocky, pock-marked dictator. Osip Mandelstam once confessed that he had Molotov in mind when he wrote these lines in his poem on Stalin – a poem, incidentally, that would cost him his life:

> Around him a rabble of thin-necked leaders –
> fawning half-men for him to play with.[4]

And Mandelstam's widow later wrote, 'Osip had noticed Molotov's thin neck – it stuck up out of his collar and was crowned by his little head.'[5]

As early as 1930–31, during the introduction of collectivization and the forcible expulsion of the rich (and not a few of the poor and middle-ranking) peasants, Molotov travelled to various districts as a special functionary invested with unlimited powers. In 1932 he played a particularly sinister part in the Ukraine, where he directed the state grain-procurement operations in the southern provinces; after his intervention the southern Ukraine was gripped by a terrible famine that carried off millions.

Molotov also played an active role in the execution of the mass terror of 1937–38. Of the twenty-five Commissars in the Council of Peoples' Commissars in 1935, the only ones to survive the terror were Mikoyan, Voroshilov, Kaganovich, M. M. Litvinov – and, of course, Molotov. Of the twenty-eight people who constituted the Council of Peoples' Commissars at the beginning of 1928, twenty were soon liquidated. And Molotov was no idle spectator of the dreadful 'meat-grinder'. He gave Stalin, Yezhov and Beria a willing hand to help turn it. It was he who read the long speech at the Central Committee Plenum of February–March 1937 that called on the entire Party membership to reinforce the struggle against the 'saboteurs' and 'spies' inside the Party – by which he meant those 'saboteurs' who tucked their Party cards safely in their pockets and shouted more loudly than everyone else that they were defending the Party's interests and the Party line. The speech was printed as a pamphlet under the title *The Lessons of the Sabotage, Wrecking and Espionage Activities of the Japanese–German–Trotskyist Agents*. Molotov frequently appended his own signature to that of Stalin on the blacklists they drew up, often adding obscene abuse of those condemned. He was behind many of the arrests of workers in the Council of Peoples' Commissars, and it was he who demanded the arrests of G. I. Lomov, K. V. Ukhanov and the First Secretary of the Urals oblast Party committee, I. A. Kabanov, as well as those of many other chairmen of oblast executive committees. There were occasions when instead of recommending a prison sentence Molotov would write alongside the names the ominous initials VMN (the initials of *vysshaya mera nakazaniya,* or 'highest form of punishment'), which in those days meant instant death by shooting.

In 1937 the first All-Union Congress of Architects took place in Moscow. According to Academician S. Ye. Chernyshev, who was a member of a delegation of architects from the Congress that visited Molotov, one of the group began to criticize buildings that had been designed by the German architect Ernst Mey, who had been working in the Soviet Union as a specialist. 'It's a pity we let him out,' Molotov mused. 'We ought to have put him inside for a ten-year stretch.'

Molotov wielded enormous power in the 1930s. His fiftieth birthday in March 1940 was marked by the bestowing of the highest orders and decorations and greetings from every corner of the land. And that was not all: the biggest industrial centre of the country, the city of Perm, was renamed Molotov, and the

Stalin in 1938.

Opposite: Voroshilov during the civil war, c. 1919. *Above:* Stalin and Voroshilov at a conference in 1936. *Below: Stalin and Voroshilov on the Kremlin Wall,* painting by Gerasimov, 1938. (Voroshilov was in fact considerably taller than Stalin.)

Photomontage by El Lisitsky, 1937. Top row, left to right: Kaganovich, Molotov, Stalin, Voroshilov, Kalinin.

Bottom row: Andreyev, Mikoyan, Postyshev, Kosior, Zhdanov, Yezhov.

Above: Voroshilov, Stalin and Mikoyan, with Kaganovich in the background, at a conference of Stakhanovites, 1936. *Below: A Memorable Meeting,* painting by Yefanov, 1936. Stalin meets the wives of engineers and technicians in heavy industry. In the background are Molotov, Mikoyan, Khrushchev, Kaganovich, Voroshilov and Budyonny; front left, Ordzhonikidze; front right, Kalinin and Krupskaya, Lenin's wife. *Opposite:* Kaganovich.

Opposite: Molotov signs the Stalin–Hitler pact, August 1939. Von Ribbentrop and Stalin look on. *Above:* Funeral of Ordzhonikidze, 1937. Pall-bearers (left to right) are Voroshilov, Molotov, Kaganovich and Stalin. *Below:* Molotov meets Hitler in Berlin, 1940.

For the Good of the Nation, painting by Nalbandyan, 1948. Members of the Politburo study plans for the afforestation of steppe regions to protect the south of Russia from drought.

Left to right: Shvernik, Bulganin, Mikoyan, Molotov, Khrushchev, Stalin, Andreyev, Beria, (?) Minister of Forestry, Voroshilov, Malenkov, Kaganovich.

Above: Stalin and Malenkov. *Below:* Malenkov and Beria on the Lenin Mausoleum, early 1950s. *Opposite:* Mikoyan.

Above: May Day on the Lenin Mausoleum, c. 1947. Left to right: Krylov, Voronov, Vasilievsky, Meretskov, Konev, Vershinin, Govorov, Voroshilov, Stalin, Bulganin, Molotov, Malenkov, Beria, Kaganovich, Popov, Zhdanov, Mikoyan, Shvernik, Voznesensky, Suslov.

Below: Government and Party leaders at the bier of Stalin in the Hall of Columns, Moscow, 6 March 1953. Front row, left to right: Molotov, Kaganovich, Bulganin, Voroshilov, Beria, Malenkov. Back row, first and second from left: Khrushchev and Mikoyan. *Over:* Mikhail Andreyevich Suslov.

map of the USSR suddenly sprouted two Molotovsks, one Molotovabad, Cape Molotov and Molotov Peak, as well as thousands of Molotov kolkhozes (collective farms), enterprises and institutes.

As a member of the Politburo and chairman of the Council of Peoples' Commissars, Molotov had to deal with various questions of foreign policy in the 1930s. He frequently disagreed with the views and proposals of M. M. Litvinov, the Peoples' Commissar for Foreign Affairs, and their relations were witnessed by a former department head in the Foreign Affairs Commissariat, E. A. Gnedin, who has written of them as follows:

> In his book on Litvinov the American writer [A. U.] Pope, expresses the completely ridiculous idea that Litvinov himself suggested 'his friend' Molotov as his successor in the job. Even though Litvinov never referred to their relations, it was nevertheless well known that they were bad. Litvinov could have had no respect for a small-minded intriguer and accomplice in terror like Molotov. And Molotov, for his part, had no love for Litvinov, who was the one People's Commissar who had preserved his independence and dignity. Molotov's hostility towards Litvinov was felt in the central diplomatic apparatus, incidentally, as young diplomatists complained that their salaries were lower than those of corresponding grades in other Commissariats.[6]

On the removal of M. M. Litvinov in May 1939 it was Molotov who became the new People's Commissar for Foreign Affairs, while still remaining head of the Soviet Government. He was identified in Stalin's entourage as a supporter of *rapprochement* between the USSR and Germany. Two years before, in 1937, the head of the Soviet trade delegation in Berlin, D. V. Kandelaki, had had talks on behalf of Stalin and Molotov with Hitler's adviser, Minister Schacht, about the improvement of political and economic relations between Germany and the USSR. These talks went on behind the back of the Soviet Commissar for Foreign Affairs.[7] Therefore Molotov's appointment as Foreign Commissar was taken as an invitation to Germany to enter into talks, a development that ought to have been regarded as unacceptable, since Hitler was hastening to make war on Poland. Following an exchange of telegrams between Hitler and Stalin, the German delegation, headed by Ribbentrop, arrived in Moscow on 23 August 1939. After brief talks, led on the Soviet side by Stalin and Molotov, the treaty of non-aggression between the USSR and Germany, together with several secret protocols, were signed on behalf of the Soviet Union by Molotov; they have gone down in history as the Molotov–Ribbentrop Pact. On 31 August, following a report by Molotov, an extraordinary session of the Supreme Soviet of the USSR ratified the treaty, and on the next day the Second World War began.

The Soviet people listened to Molotov telling them on the radio of the Red Army's invasion of the western Ukraine and western Belorussia. On 29 September 1939 Molotov signed the German–Soviet Boundary and Friendship Treaty. One of the secret protocols of this treaty spoke of the prohibition on Soviet territory of anti-Fascist and anti-Hitler propaganda. Speaking at yet another extraordinary session of the Supreme Soviet, Molotov said:

> The ideology of Hitlerism, like any other ideological system, can be either accepted or rejected – it is a matter of political view. But everyone will agree that an ideology cannot be destroyed by force. . . . Therefore it is both senseless and criminal to wage a war 'for the liquidation of Hitlerism' while flourishing above it the false flag of the struggle for democracy.[8]

Soon after Molotov became Foreign Commissar many Soviet diplomats – senior workers in the Foreign Commissariat as well as ambassadors and consuls in various countries – were arrested, clearly with his sanction. Among those arrested was E. A. Gnedin, then director of a department in the Foreign Commissariat, who sent a long declaration to Molotov from the Lubyanka prison. In his recently published memoirs he writes:

> It is uncomfortable to admit it, but at that time I still had not lost hope that an appeal to the chairman of the Sovnarkom,

composed in a resolute tone, might bring a favourable outcome to the affair. I did not expect that Molotov himself was involved in the progress of the case, and I thought that a statement from prison would at least be registered somewhere and perhaps even taken into account. Later I realized that our complaints and statements from prison and camp had no effect at all. After returning to Moscow I learned from a former employee in Molotov's secretariat not only that Molotov never responded to statements from innocent people in incarceration – he did not even read them – but also that he forbade such statements to be registered as incoming documents. We had been categorized as expendable, and our declarations of innocence were filed in the waste-paper basket.[9]

Nazi Germany was not punctilious in her observation of the treaties and agreements that she made with the USSR. The appearance of German troops in Finland and Romania caused alarm in the Soviet Union, and in the autumn of 1940 Stalin dispatched Molotov to Berlin for more talks. It was Molotov's dubious honour to be the only Soviet political leader ever to shake Hitler's hand. But the talks in the Berlin Reichskanzlei came to nothing. Hitler refused to negotiate over questions that particularly troubled the Soviet leadership; instead he proposed they discuss the Soviet Union's joining the 'anti-Comintern pact' and the dismemberment of the British Empire. Molotov went home empty-handed. Like Stalin, he ignored the enormous number of facts that testified to Hitler's preparations for an invasion of the USSR. When the Germans attacked Molotov summoned the German ambassador, Schulenburg, who delivered Germany's formal declaration of war, upon which Molotov managed to mutter the lame phrase, 'What did we do to deserve this?'

It was in a short radio speech at noon on 22 June 1941 that Molotov informed the Soviet people of Germany's invasion of the USSR and the outbreak of war. He ended with the words, 'Our cause is just. The enemy will be beaten. Victory will be ours.' Every Soviet citizen of the older generation remembers those words. In almost all the memoirs of the period one finds accounts of the circumstances in which the writer recalls hearing that speech and learning of the outbreak of war. Many people wondered why it was Molotov and not Stalin who made the announcement. But there was little time for wondering: the war was already under way.

Stalin had become chairman of the Soviet of People's Commissars on 6 May 1941, with Molotov as his deputy. Molotov also became Stalin's deputy in the all-powerful State Defence Committee when it first came into being after the outbreak of the war. His chief task in the State Defence Committee was diplomacy, negotiating with the political leaders of Britain, the USA and other countries. In 1942 he travelled to London to conclude the Anglo–Soviet Military Alliance, and for the same purpose he went to Washington, where he met President Roosevelt and the military and diplomatic leadership of the USA.

Only once did he have to deal with strictly military matters. In October 1941, after the Germans had broken through at Vyazma, Molotov and Voroshilov were sent by the State Defence Committee to the Gzhatsk and Mozhaisk district, where they had been instructed to assess the gravity of the situation and to make recommendations about how to localize the German breakthrough. Molotov was not much use on that trip; suggestions for concrete measures were in fact put forward by a group of staff officers led by A. M. Vasilevsky.

In the first weeks of the war bottles filled with inflammable liquid were deployed against German tanks. At first chemical units in the regiments and divisions made them up, using simply petrol and some additives, but then the bottles began to arrive from the rear as ammunition. They were made in every sort of workshop, even lemonade factories, and the mixture varied. The Germans nicknamed these bottles 'Molotov Cocktails', a name that did not please the Soviet Army but is still used in the West. It had not been Molotov's idea to supply the troops with this particular weapon, although the order for the mass production of the bottles as an anti-tank weapon was signed by him as deputy chairman of the State Defence Committee. Perhaps that was how they got their nickname.

In *A Man called Intrepid*,[10] a book about Western intelligence operations during the war, William Stevenson alleges that in

1943 Molotov travelled 300 kilometres behind the enemy lines in order to discuss a separate peace with the German leadership. This fact was unknown to us. We did know, however, that he took part in the inter-Allied conferences: Teheran in 1943, Yalta and Potsdam in 1945. The subjects discussed were the co-ordination of the war effort and the post-war structure of Germany, Poland and the Balkan Peninsula. Before the war ended the USA, the USSR, Britain and China had agreed on the creation of an organization of states to guard the peace once hostilities ceased. Talks on this question took place in 1944–45 and resulted in the Charter of the United Nations. The Charter was signed in San Francisco on behalf of the Soviet Union by V. M. Molotov.

In the 1920s Molotov had played an active role in the work of the Communist International (Comintern), at first under the leadership of G. Ye. Zinoviev and N. I. Bukharin and later under that of Stalin. He was a member of the Soviet delegation at all the later Comintern congresses. In 1943 it fell to him to hold talks, in Stalin's name, with Roosevelt and Churchill on the liquidation of Comintern and the legalization of the Russian Orthodox Church.

Among Russian émigrés in the West, and even among sovietologists, the opinion has been expressed for many years that Stalin turned to the Orthodox Church for support after the heavy defeats of 1941. Stalin is presumed to have wanted to exploit the national and religious sentiments of the Soviet people rather than to rely on their socialist patriotism. This view is mistaken, however. On 3 July 1941 Stalin gave a speech in which he called for the defence of the national culture and of the statehood of not only the Russian people but all the peoples of the USSR; proclaimed the inviolability of Soviet authority; and urged the need to rally round the Soviet Government and the 'Party of Lenin and Stalin'. Nor did he say a word about the Church in a speech of 6 November 1941, calling instead for the strengthening of the union of the workers, the peasants and all the peoples of the USSR and, once again, the defence of socialism. That day's solemn session ended with the singing of the 'Internationale'.

By the end of the 1930s the Russian Orthodox Church was to all intents and purposes a shattered institution. The priests and hierarchs that had survived in Moscow were evacuated, some of them to Ulyanovsk, and nobody in Moscow's governing circles gave them a thought throughout the whole of 1942. However, in the second half of 1943 – that is to say, after the victory at Stalingrad, the defeat of the Germans on many fronts and the battles on the Kursk Arc, when it seemed to many observers that Soviet victory over the Germans was assured – the Soviet Union's Western allies began to feel uneasy at the prospect of the Red Army's presence in Western Europe. It was necessary to reassure Roosevelt and Churchill and to prove to them that at that time the USSR was contemplating not 'world revolution' but simply the defeat of German Fascism. To this end the decision was taken to do a little window-dressing, to stage what was in effect a cosmetic operation. Stalin was sure that he would be able to maintain control over the activities of all Communist Parties after the war, as he had before. As far as the Church was concerned, he had no intention whatever of restoring it to its former position. It was a fact that the partial restoration of the Church's rights was a palliative, a response to the grief of millions of people who had lost their fathers, sons and husbands in the war and who looked to the Church for the consolation that it could give – but to Stalin this was of secondary importance.

The decision to liquidate Comintern had already been taken in May 1943; without any doubt it was meant as a concession to the Soviet Union's Western allies, though it also corresponded with Stalin's own desire, as he had never shown much concern with or sympathy for Comintern. The essential changes in the Church's position were made in the autumn of 1943. I possess documentary evidence of the meeting that took place between Stalin and Molotov and leaders of the Orthodox Church. The evidence varies somewhat in the detail but not in the essence of the matter. The most accurate account is given, in my view, by A. E. Levitin-Krasnov, who was in Ulyanovsk in 1943 and was well acquainted with a number of prominent churchmen. He writes:

By 3 September Metropolitan Sergius and his retainers, Kolch-
itsky and his family and Ioann Razumov, were already on the
train. Their departure had been so rushed that they had not even
had time to pack and had only managed to grab essentials. . . .
Events unfolded with cinematic speed. Early next morning the
train was in Moscow. The Metropolitan was met at the station
by Metropolitan Aleksii (the future Patriarch), who had arrived
from Leningrad in similar haste, and by Metropolitan Nikolai of
Kiev. . . . Surprise followed surprise. The Metropolitan was
taken not to the residence on Bauman Street where he had lived
for fifteen years but to a luxurious mansion on Chistaya
Street, which had been the private residence of the German
ambassador, Count Schulenburg, before the war. . . . It was
announced on the morning of 4 September that there would be a
visit to the Kremlin that evening. A government car arrived at
Chistaya Street at 9 p.m., and Metropolitans Sergius, Aleksii and
Nikolai were duly seated in it. Ten minutes later the car drove
into the Kremlin, and in another ten minutes they entered a
spacious, wood-panelled office, in which two people were
seated at a table, Stalin and Molotov. Everyone shook hands and
sat down. Molotov opened the conversation with the
announcement that the Soviet government, and Comrade Stalin
in particular, wished to know the Church's requirements.
Metropolitans Aleksii and Nikolai maintained a confused
silence. Suddenly Metropolitan Sergius began to speak. . . .
Calmly, with a slight stammer, he spoke in the manner of a man
who is accustomed to discussing serious matters with people in
the highest places. (When Stalin was still a seminary student,
Metropolitan Sergius was already a bishop and rector of the
Petersburg Religious Academy.)

The Metropolitan pointed to the need for widespread reopen-
ing of churches, the present number of which was totally
inadequate to meet the spiritual needs of the people. He also
argued that it was important to convene the Synod and to hold
elections for a Patriarch. Finally he put the case for a large
number of seminaries, as the Church lacked priests. At this point
Stalin suddenly broke his silence. 'Why haven't you any
personnel? Where have they got to?' he asked, taking his pipe
out of his mouth and staring intently at the company. Aleksii
and Nikolai were confused . . . everyone knew that the
'personnel' were scattered in the camps. But Metropolitan
Sergius was not discountenanced. . . . The old man replied, 'We

lack personnel for several reasons, one of which is that we train a man to be a priest, but he becomes a Marshal of the Soviet Union.' A satisfied grin moved the dictator's moustache. He said, 'Yes, yes, I was a seminarist. I even heard about you.' He then fell to reminiscing about his years as a seminarist. . . . He said that his mother had regretted to her dying day that he had not become a priest. The conversation between the metropolitan and the dictator took on a relaxed air. After tea had been served, they talked business.

Their discussion lasted until three in the morning. Besides Stalin and Molotov, a group of technical experts took part. One could call this meeting historical in the fullest sense of the word. It resulted in the working out of the Statute of the Russian Church and of the conditions in which the Church has functioned to the present day. To be sure, the order provokes a great deal of censure today, but in those days, after decades of terror which had been directed against the Church, the new order undoubtedly appeared to be a step forward, as it allowed for the possibility of the Orthodox Church's legal existence.

At the end of the conversation the ancient and ailing metropolitan was exhausted. . . . Stalin took him by the arm with great care like a real subdeacon, led him down the stairs and bade him farewell in the following words: 'My Lord, that is as much as I can do for you at the present time!' And with that, he wished the hierarchs goodbye.

A few days later the Synod of bishops was convened at the house on Chistaya Street – it was not difficult to arrange, since at that time there were only seventeen bishops in the Russian Church – and on Sunday, 12 September (Alexander Nevsky Day), in the Yelokhov Cathedral of the Epiphany, Metropolitan Sergius was enthroned. . . . After an eighteen-year gap, the Russian Church was once again crowned with a Patriarch.[11]

In the years following the war the conduct of Soviet foreign policy remained Molotov's chief occupation, though he was not well suited to work in the diplomatic field. On several occasions he had to go to New York to take part in the work of the United Nations. The speeches he made at the General Assembly were of his usual kind – detailed, dry, boring. The allies and supporters of the United States had a majority at that time, and as he frequently had to resort to the Soviet right of veto in the Security Council, he acquired the nickname 'Mr Nyet' in UN circles. His responsibilities included maintaining links with the NKVD–MGB on questions of intelligence.

It goes without saying that as a Politburo member Molotov also bears responsibility for all the repressions of the post-war years: for the 'Leningrad Affair', for the arrest of practically all the members of the Anti-Fascist Committee of Soviet Jews and for the expulsions of many Soviet nationalities from their national territories that had taken place earlier. A victim of one of those repressive campaigns was none other than Molotov's own wife, Polina Semyonovna Zhemchuzhina.

Polina Semyonovna had joined the Party in 1918, when she was still a young girl; only a few years later she was running the women's section of a Party provincial committee in the Ukraine. She was attending a congress of women's sections in Moscow in the early 1920s when she became very ill and had to be rushed to hospital. As the man responsible for running the congress, Molotov decided to visit the sick delegate – and returned several times. When she had recovered she remained in Moscow and became his wife. Their daughter, Svetlana, was born not long after.

At the Kremlin Polina became very friendly with Stalin's wife, Nadezhda Alliluyeva. The young women met often and were quite open with each other; it was no secret to Polina that Stalin's marriage was going from bad to worse. On the fateful night of 15 November 1932, when Stalin was openly rude to his wife during dinner at Voroshilov's, she left the apartment in indignation accompanied by Polina, who spent a long time trying to calm her. When Nadezhda was found in her bedroom next morning, shot through the head and with a pistol in her hand, it was only after G. K. Ordzhonikidze, his wife Zinaida, Molotov and Polina had been called to the scene that Stalin was awakened with the news of his wife's suicide.

To Stalin, vengeful and suspicious, Polina Semyonovna was instantly *persona non grata,* but he knew how to wait and to hide his feelings. The purges of the 1930s passed Polina by – indeed, she held responsible jobs in the Council of People's Commissars in the second half of the 1930s. For a short time she was

deputy People's Commissar for Food Production, People's
Commissar for Fisheries and head of the Cosmetics Industry
Board, and at the Eighteenth Party Congress she was elected a
candidate member of the Central Committee.

Polina Semyonovna was Jewish, and when the Anti-Fascist
Committee of Soviet Jews was founded during the Second
World War she became a leading member. Its chairman was the
old Bolshevik and Central Committee member S. A.
Lozovsky, who was also head of the Soviet Information
Bureau. Like most of the other anti-Fascist committees (for
example, that of Soviet Women), the Anti-Fascist Committee
of Soviet Jews was liquidated after the war. In 1948 the Jewish
state of Israel was created by a United Nations resolution with
the active support of the Soviet Union. Indeed, the USSR was
the first state to establish diplomatic relations with Israel, and
Golda Meir soon arrived in Moscow as the first Israeli
ambassador. Naturally, the members of the Anti-Fascist Committee of Soviet Jews were invited to receptions held at the
Israeli Embassy, and Golda Meir and Polina Semyonovna had
frequent chats. Moreover, Polina Semyonovna had a sister who
had emigrated to Israel (or Palestine, as it then was) during the
civil war and with whom she had kept up correspondence until
1939, so if Molotov had ever had to fill in a form which
included a question about relations abroad, he would have had
to mention his wife's sister and nephew.

The cordial relations between Israel and the Soviet Union did
not last very long, however, as in 1948–49 the notorious
campaign against 'rootless cosmopolitans' gathered force, and
the mass repression of all Jewish social and national organizations began. This was a good moment for Stalin to settle the
score with the woman who had once been his wife's close friend
and who, in his view, knew too much. Naturally, this was not
the charge that was brought against her openly.

Polina Semyonovna was accused of 'treason against the
Motherland' through her links with international Zionism and
so on. The question of her arrest was discussed by the
Politburo. After Beria had presented the facts collected by his
agencies, all the members of the Politburo voted for her arrest

except Molotov, who abstained, although he did not speak in her defence.

Returning home that night, Molotov was obliged to tell his wife about the Politburo's decision and her imminent arrest.

'And you believed all that slander?' screamed his distraught wife.

'But they produced all those convincing documents,' replied the sad and confused Molotov.

They arrested his wife the next day. The former General Secretary of the Israeli Communist Party, S. Mikunis, describes a curious meeting he had with Molotov in 1955:

> It took place in the Kremlin Hospital at Kuntsevo, where I had been sent after having been slightly unwell. . . . Quite unexpectedly, one day I ran into Molotov in one of the corridors. I had seen him only once before, when he made a speech in Paris at the Friends of Peace Congress. . . . Like me, he was now in hospital pyjamas but, despite that, he still had that arrogant look of his, that severe, unapproachable expression on his face. I went up to him and asked, 'How could you, a member of the Politburo, let them arrest your wife?' He gave me a cold look and asked me who I thought I was. I replied, 'I am the General Secretary of the Israeli Communist Party, and that's why I'm asking you – and not only you: I'm going to ask the Central Committee too. Why did you let them arrest Polina Zhem-chuzhina?' Without moving a muscle in his steely face, he replied, 'Because I am a member of the Politburo and I must obey Party discipline. . . . I submitted to the Politburo, which had decided that my wife must be put away.' That was an odd little scene for you![12]

In 1949 Stalin was ill frequently and for long periods. Problems that could not be shelved fell to Molotov to solve, in consultation, of course, with the other members of the Polit-buro. In December 1949, on Stalin's seventieth birthday, each member of the Politburo was required to publish a long article singing the praises of the 'leader and teacher', and Molotov was first in line. A few months later it was Molotov's own sixtieth birthday. He was awarded his fourth Order of Lenin – in 1943 he had been made a Hero of Socialist Labour – and he was elected an Honorary Member of the Soviet Academy of Sciences. A few more settlements and Central Asian villages appeared on the map under the name Molotov. The house where the Skryabins had lived in Nolinsk – renamed Molotovsk – was turned into a museum. Yet while nearly all Western observers continued to regard Molotov as second only to Stalin in the Soviet and Party hierarchy, it was precisely during that period that he gradually fell into disfavour. The arrest of his wife was only one sign of Stalin's distrust. In 1949 he was abruptly relieved of his duties as Minister of Foreign Affairs, and his place was taken by A. Ya. Vyshinsky, a man who had long before established himself as a master of demagogic rhetoric. Vyshinsky had received a fine training in that skill during the show trials of 'enemies of the people' in the 1930s, when he had played the part of Prosecutor General of the USSR. It was from the dais of the UN General Assembly that Vyshinsky's speeches now began to ring out.

Molotov remained a member of the Politburo and Stalin's deputy in the Council of Ministers, but he was given important missions by Stalin less and less frequently. Stalin soon stopped inviting him to his dacha, where, over dinners and suppers often lasting until after midnight, important matters of state were decided. Khrushchev recalls that on occasion the members of the Politburo themselves would invite Molotov to join them, and that this greatly angered Stalin, who in the end simply forbade them to include Molotov. On one occasion Stalin expressed a suspicion, in Khrushchev's presence, that Molotov had been recruited on one of his trips abroad and was working as an 'agent of American imperialism'. Stalin wanted to find out, through Vyshinsky who was then in the USA, how Molotov had travelled round the country during his stay in America – whether he had had a special separate railway carriage to himself, as if that would have been an important detail to be used against him. Many of the people who were under arrest at that time were forced to give false testimony against Molotov, as well as against Kaganovich, Voroshilov and Mikoyan. Nevertheless, at the Nineteenth Party Congress in 1952 not only was Molotov a member of the small Congress presidium but he even opened the proceedings with a brief introductory speech. At the end of the Congress he was appointed to the Party Central Committee and the Presidium of the Party Central Committee, enlarged, according to Stalin's wishes, to thirty-six members and candidates.

For the permanent direction of Party affairs Stalin proposed the appointment of a Bureau of the Presidium and dictated a list of nine names – Molotov's was not among them. In Central Committee circles people started to regard him as a doomed man. There were numerous signs after the Nineteenth Congress that Stalin wanted to launch a new terroristic purge of the Party higher ranks; there were also indications that one of the first victims of such a purge would be Molotov.

Stalin's advancing physical decrepitude was clear enough to those close to him, but his death took both the country and the upper ranks of the Party completely by surprise. It was hard to accept that the man who had been looked upon as a god could die from a brain haemorrhage or from heart failure. Both people and Party had become so accustomed to the need for a leader that the question arose immediately of who was going to take his place. Not surprisingly, Molotov's name came up more often than others. Khrushchev himself wrote later in his *Memoirs:* 'All of us who belonged to the pre-war leadership regarded Molotov as the future leader who would replace Stalin. . . .'[13] It was not merely Molotov's high standing in the Party that Khrushchev had in mind but also the fact that he was the best-known Party and political figure after Stalin.

Not that anyone was actually comparing Molotov with Stalin. I was working at that time as a teacher in a workers' settlement in the Urals, and I recall that the day after Stalin died a group of local teachers came to see me. They had all fought at the front during the war. One of them, very drunk, was weeping. 'Who are we going to fight for now?' he kept whining. 'We died for Stalin, but what now? For Molotov? No thanks, I'm not going to go out and die for Molotov!' Among ex-soldiers and officers Molotov clearly enjoyed no popularity whatsoever.

Next day, however, we read in our newspapers that the post

of chairman of the Council of Ministers, which was at that time regarded as the highest post, was to be occupied by G. M. Malenkov, and that Molotov, Beria, Bulganin and Kaganovich were to be his deputies. Malenkov, Molotov and Beria gave speeches at Stalin's funeral, and in all official announcements the names of the leaders were given in the following order: Malenkov, Beria, Molotov, Voroshilov, Khrushchev, Bulganin, Kaganovich, Mikoyan. In his funeral speech Molotov said, among other things:

> We can justly be proud that for the last thirty years we have lived and worked under the guidance of Stalin. . . . We are pupils of Lenin and Stalin. And we will always remember what Stalin taught us right up to the end of his days. . . . The whole life of this inspired national fighter for communism, illuminated as it was by the sunshine of great ideas, is a vital and life-affirming example to us all.[14]

Molotov became a member of the newly constituted, smaller Presidium (formerly the Politburo) of the Party Central Committee and was appointed Foreign Minister once again.

Soon after Stalin's death men and women began to be rehabilitated and released from the prison camps. The first was possibly A. Ya. Kapler, the screen writer who had been arrested during the war because of his association with Svetlana Alliluyeva. (Stalin had been opposed to their marriage.) Kapler was released on 6 March 1953. It happened that the day of Stalin's funeral, 9 March, was also Molotov's birthday. As they were leaving the mausoleum, Khrushchev and Malenkov wished him a happy birthday, despite the occasion, and asked what he would like as a present. 'Give me back Polina,' he replied coldly and moved on. Beria was immediately informed of Molotov's request. Beria in any case knew that it no longer made sense to hold Molotov's wife a prisoner. In 1949 she had been sentenced to a few years of exile, but in January 1953 she had been brought back in Moscow, having been included among the 'participants' in a 'Zionist conspiracy' together with a group of Jewish doctors and the late S. M. Mikhoels, a leading Yiddish actor and theatre director who was prominent in the war-time Anti-Fascist Committee of Soviet Jews and who had died in a car accident staged by the secret police. She had been interrogated under torture. The interrogations had only ceased on 1 or 2 March, yet on 9 or 10 March she was summoned to Beria's office. She had not heard that Stalin was dead and feared the worst. But Beria immediately got up from behind his desk, embraced his visitor and exclaimed, 'Polina! You are an honoured Communist!' She fell to the floor in a dead faint. She was quickly revived, allowed to rest for a while, given new clothes and driven home to her dacha and to Molotov – an unusual birthday present.

When Khrushchev and Malenkov – taking steps to ensure maximum security – began to discuss with the rest of the leadership the question of Beria's arrest, Molotov gave them his support. A year later he supported Khrushchev and Bulganin at a Central Committee plenum at which various accusations were made against Malenkov, notably for his poor performance in handling agriculture, on which, in Stalin's last years, it had been his responsibility to report to the Politburo. Molotov also accused Malenkov of underestimating the essential develop-ment of heavy industry. As a result, Malenkov was relieved of his duties as Chairman of the Council of Ministers, and his place was taken by N. A. Bulganin. Molotov and Khrushchev were politically and temperamentally too far apart for their alliance to last long, however.

Khrushchev's influence over the new leadership of the country and the Party was pre-eminent by the end of 1954. The leadership changed not only in content but also in style, and a whole host of new initiatives and proposals was discussed in the Presidium of the Central Committee. Khrushchev's dominance was evident not only in the conduct of internal affairs but also in foreign policy, a fact that greatly irritated Molotov, who was still Foreign Minister as well as a member of the Presidium.

During the debates on Khrushchev's proposals for the opening up of the virgin lands Molotov and Voroshilov had raised several objections, and they had also criticized the draft decree on the new agricultural planning arrangements. In ad-dition, Molotov had opposed the unconditional 'rehabilitation' of Tito, who was, as far as he was concernced, if not a Fascist, then at least a revisionist. For this reason, the preliminary talks on the normalization of relations with Yugoslavia took place without the involvement of the Foreign Ministry, and Molotov did not accompany Khrushchev and Bulganin on their visit to Tito in May 1955. Believing that the USSR was conceding too much to the West and not receiving enough by way of compensation, Molotov did much to hamper the conclusion of the Austrian State Treaty and the normalization of relations with Japan. He did not accompany Khrushchev and Bulganin on their trip to India and Burma in 1955. His conservatism in foreign policy, particularly in connection with the Yugoslav question, was subjected to criticism at the July 1955 plenum of the Party Central Committee.

His role as a theoretician also came under attack in the same year. At a session of the Supreme Soviet he made a speech in which he said that the 'foundations of a socialist society' had been laid in the USSR. This prompted a salvo of objections from other members of the Central Committee, who protested that the 'foundations of socialism' had been laid in the 1930s and that now, in the mid-1950s, it was socialist society itself that had been constructed. Molotov was closer the truth than his opponents, of course, but he nevertheless lost the dogmatic argument and was forced to confess his error publicly. In a 'Letter to the Editor' published in the journal *Kommunist* he declared:

> I consider the formulation that I presented at a session of the Supreme Soviet of the USSR on 8 February 1955, on the question of the building of socialist society in the USSR, from which it is possible to draw the conclusion that only the foundations of a socialist society have been built, to be theoretically erroneous and politically dangerous.[15]

The Twentieth Party Congress of 1956 and Khrushchev's secret speech, 'On Overcoming the Cult of Personality and its Consequences', widened still further the divergence between Khrushchev and Molotov, who on that occasion was supported by such people as Kaganovich, Malenkov, Voroshilov and some others. In practice Molotov was no longer carrying out his basic duties as Foreign Minister. He was not included in the government delegation that visited England in March 1956, nor had he been to China with Khrushchev earlier. Then in the middle of 1956, no more than a day before the start of Tito's visit to the USSR, he was relieved of his duties as Foreign Minister. He remained, however, a member of the Presidium of the Party's Central Committee and deputy chairman of the Council of Ministers. Around him there gradually formed a group of malcontents who comprised the majority of the Presidium of the Party Central Committee. It was a series of errors committed by Khrushchev that provoked this situation, in particular his over-hasty liquidation of the industrial Ministries and their replacement by Oblast Economic Councils (*Sovnarkhozy*) and his launching of the slogan calling for a threefold increase in meat production within three or four years.

On the anniversary of Lenin's birthday, 22 April 1957, *Pravda* carried a long article by Molotov entitled 'On Lenin'. The point was driven home in the article that Molotov was the only member of the Presidium of the Party Central Committee who had worked directly under Lenin's guidance and that he had had meetings with Lenin from as early as April 1917. Molotov referred to Stalin's crimes as 'mistakes': 'We know that mistakes, sometimes very serious mistakes, are inevitable when such vast and complex historical tasks are being resolved. There are not and cannot be any guarantees given on this score by anyone.' According to Molotov, the Party's policy as a whole had always been correct and 'faithful to the banner of Leninism'.

Meanwhile, Khrushchev's opponents continued to meet and talk in strict secrecy. They proposed that Molotov be appointed First Secretary of the Central Committee and that Khrushchev be given the post of Minister of Agriculture or some other task on condition that he relinquish voluntarily his position as head of the Party. Should he refuse to submit to the majority of the Presidium, his arrest was not to be ruled out. Events, however, took a different turn.

The decisive clash between Khrushchev and Molotov took

place in June 1957, at a session of the Presidium of the Party's Central Committee. Molotov's group was in the majority and included N. A Bulganin, M. G. Pervukhin, M. Z. Saburov and D. T. Shepilov, in addition to Kaganovich, Malenkov and Voroshilov. But Molotov had miscalculated. He did not have behind him the majority of the full Central Committee, which was convened by Khrushchev's supporters. Nor did he have the support of the KGB, headed by I. A. Serov, or of the Army, headed by G. K. Zhukov. The majority of the Party Central Committee feared that if Molotov were to assume power, there would be renewed repression of the Party and state apparatus. The defeat of Molotov's group at the June plenum of the Central Committee was so thoroughgoing that even his own supporters voted to accept the resolution condemning their activity. Only Molotov himself abstained from voting.

The plenum removed Molotov, Kaganovich, Malenkov and Shepilov from the Presidium and also excluded them from the Central Committee of the Party. This was the only occasion in the history of the Party on which the Central Committee had not submitted to a decision of its Presidium (i.e. the Politburo) and even rescinded that decision. The political career of V. M. Molotov was to all intents and purposes at an end.

Molotov and his close allies feared that after the June plenum of the Central Committee they would be arrested, but Khrushchev refrained from taking that step, nor did he even insist on expelling the 'factionalists' from the Party. Indeed, Molotov was given a relatively important assignment: he was appointed Soviet ambassador to Mongolia. His work in Mongolia did not demand any great effort, however, and as in his earlier years he had aspired to the role not only of politician but also of Marxist–Leninist theoretician, so now in Mongolia he resumed his theoretical studies. He followed sedulously everything that went on in Moscow, and he was not afraid to share his views with the occasional visitors who came to the embassy in Ulan-Bator. In 1958, for example, in conversation with a Soviet delegation to the Mongolian capital, he expressed his doubts about the wisdom of disbanding the Machine-Tractor Stations (MTS) too speedily. (His criticism, incidentally, was quite justified, as the dismantling of the MTS, executed with excessive haste, caused great damage to the country's collective farms.) During the preparations for Lenin's ninetieth anniversary in 1960 Molotov sent a long article to *Kommunist* entitled 'On Vladimir Ilyich Lenin'. It was not published, however, as it contained a number of historical and doctrinal mistakes.

As Mongolia borders on China, on every possible occasion the Chinese leadership made a point of demonstrating its respect for Molotov as the closest pupil and comrade-in-arms of Stalin; consequently, Khrushchev decided to move Molotov to other work, further away from the Chinese frontier. As it happened, just at that time Corresponding Member of the Academy of Sciences V. S. Yemelyanov, who was overloaded with responsibilities, was seeking to be relieved of the post of Soviet co-chairman of the United Nations International Atomic Energy Agency, whose headquarters were located in Vienna. An early decision of the Council of Ministers gave the job to Molotov – Yemelyanov remained in charge of the general direction of the delegation – and Molotov moved from Mongolia to Vienna.

During Khrushchev's meeting with the newly elected American President Kennedy in Vienna at the beginning of June 1961, among those who were invited to be present during the first meeting of the heads of Government one could see a little old gentleman in gold-rimmed pince-nez. It was Molotov, the Soviet representative at the UN Atomic Energy Agency. Khrushchev appeared and was greeted by Molotov with an inscrutable look. He flung him a casual greeting in return and moved on.

In the summer of that year active preparation was under way for the Twenty-Second Congress of the Party. A draft of the new Party Programme was published for general discussion. Only those articles were published, however, that wholly endorsed the draft Programme or suggested minor additions and alterations. Molotov decided that he would like to take part in the general debate, so shortly before the Congress he sent the Central Committee a detailed and critical analysis of the draft Programme, which he characterized as an erroneous and 'revisionist' document. His critical remarks were not published; the only account of them – brief and probably not entirely accurate – is to be found in speeches made at the Congress by P. A. Satyukov and P. N. Pospelov. The fact that Molotov had ventured any criticism of the draft Programme at all angered Khrushchev, and it was without doubt one reason for the inclusion in Khrushchev's Congress report of a special section devoted to an attack on the 'anti-Party group' of Molotov, Malenkov, Kaganovich and the other 'factionalists'. Other delegates also directed some sharp criticism at Molotov in their speeches. Stalin's crimes and those of Molotov and of Stalin's other close associates were no longer confined to secret reports; now they were the subject of speeches by delegates in open session. Many demanded that Molotov and his political allies be expelled from the Party, and indeed it was not long after the Congress that Molotov was removed from all his posts. His primary organization, where he was registered as a Party member, expelled him, and the former Soviet Prime Minister retired on his pension. As for all the towns and villages which had been given the name of Molotov, they had all reverted to their former names in 1957, and there was no longer a single enterprise or institution in the Soviet Union that bore his name.

Molotov returned to Moscow. After his expulsion from the Party he forfeited many of the privileges that he had earlier managed to retain, but his wife still had some of her own. Together with their small family, they now lived either in their apartment on Granovsky Street or at their dacha at Zhukovka, a community of villas reserved for the privileged. Apart from relations, they received very few visitors, although they were once visited by Stalin's daughter, Svetlana Alliluyeva, who has described the occasion in her book *Just One Year:*

> I saw the aged, withered Molotov, a pensioner in his little apartment, after Kosygin had replaced Khrushchev. As usual, he said very little, just 'Yes' to everything. Before I had always seen him saying 'Yes' to my father; now he was saying it to his wife. She was full of energy and fighting spirit. She had not been expelled from the Party, and now she was attending Party

meetings at the confectionery factory, just as she had done in her youth. The whole family was sitting at the table, and Polina said to me, 'Your father was a genius. He liquidated the fifth column in our country, and when the war broke out the Party and the people were one. There's no revolutionary spirit around nowadays, just opportunism everywhere. Look at what the Italian Communists are up to! It's shameful! The war scared everyone. China's our only hope. Only they have kept alive the revolutionary spirit.' Molotov said 'Yes,' and nodded his head. Their daughter and son-in-law kept quiet and stared down at their plates. They were of a different generation, and they felt ashamed. They saw their parents as excavated dinosaurs that had been petrified and preserved in a glacier.[16]

(The conversation took place while the 'cultural revolution' in China was at its height.)

Molotov and Polina were often seen together during the years 1963–7, strolling through the streets around the Arbat district, chatting away and clutching each other tightly by the arm. And then, in 1967, she died. Her funeral was organized by the factory at which her Party membership was registered. She was a long-standing Communist, and the local district committee representatives attended. Molotov gave a speech, his first and last in public since becoming a pensioner. He spoke of the path his late wife had taken and of the great work that had been achieved by the Party and the Soviet state in the 1930s and 1940s. Naturally, he said nothing about his wife's arrest and exile, nor about the crimes of the past years.

Molotov began writing his memoirs in the 1960s, working on them both at home and in the professorial reading room of the Lenin Library. (It goes almost without saying that both he and Stalin had long been dropped by the Academy of Sciences from its list of 'honorary members', but Molotov had at least retained the privilege of being allowed to use the hall reserved for professors and academicians.) Having completed the first part of his memoirs dealing with the times of the two revolutions, 1905 and 1917, he telephoned the writer B. N. Polevoy, who was chief editor of the journal *Yunost* (*Youth*), which had just published the first part of Mikoyan's memoirs, also about the revolutionary period. Polevoy did not know what to say to Molotov, however; obviously not eager to accept the offer, he asked Molotov to call him again in a few days' time. When in due course Molotov called, Polevoy told him that *Yunost* would not print his memoirs, and he advised the author to try the Marxism–Leninism Institute. It is not known if Molotov took this advice, but anyone who knows him can be sure that his memoirs contain not one word of repentance or reappraisal but simply excuses to justify his past actions.

He now lives in his apartment with his daughter Svetlana, who is a historian by profession. He has no special guard; he can come and go in Moscow as he pleases, and he can travel anywhere in the Soviet Union that takes his fancy. He has been seen frequently at exhibitions and concerts but most of all at the theatre, in particular at the Vakhtangov, where he has been to see A. Ye. Korneichuk's play *The Front* several times. In the course of the play a soldier in the trenches utters the line: 'I've written a letter to Molotov.'

He also went several times to see John Reed's *Ten Days that Shook the World*, which was staged at the Taganka. In one scene there was a disguised attack on Khrushchev – everyone saw through it – which was retained long after the ex-premier had been put out to grass by the plenum of the Central Committee at the end of 1964. Molotov very often goes to the cinema in Zhukovka that was built for the privileged inhabitants of the villas there, where they frequently show Western films that are not put on general release. In the audience there are often quite a few 'retired' people who know Molotov well, but apparently they treat him with indifference.

He has rarely met any public figures or journalists, though there have been some exceptions. For example, several times he met the writer N. F. Stadnyuk, who is regarded as a Stalinist and who wrote for the journal *Oktyabr* (*October*). Stadnyuk was working on his novel *The War*, in which he was trying to recreate the conditions of the months just before and just after the outbreak of the war – in an extraordinarily distorted way, let it be said. It is enough to mention that the novel justifies unequivocally Stalin's vicious repression of the cream of the Soviet military leadership. On several points it was Molotov himself who advised Stadnyuk. When the book appeared in 1970–71, it provoked considerable protest from both the intellectual establishment and ordinary readers. (You will also find Molotov's name mentioned quite often in A. B. Chakovsky's novels on the war and in B. Sokolov's *Invasion*.) And at one time Molotov was visited quite often by the writer Sergei Ivanovich Malashkin, his senior by two years. They had met in Nizhny-Novgorod in 1918, when the young Malashkin was just publishing his first book of poems, entitled *Muscles,* to be followed a few years later by his book *Rebellions*. The two of them had plenty to reminisce about. They were occasionally joined by another Nizhny-Novgorod writer, N. I. Kochin, who has just turned a mere 80.

Among his well-wishers Molotov can include the inveterate Albanian dictator Enver Hoxha, who, in his memoirs recently published in Tirana, says complimentary things only about Molotov when he is recalling his meetings with Soviet leaders. True, Hoxha regards Molotov as a weak character, in both a personal and a political capacity, but in Hoxha's view among the post-Stalin leadership only he merits any respect at all.

There have also been accidental meetings, of course. For instance, the well-known artist Yu. V. Nikulin was driving along in his car one day when at the side of the road he caught sight of an old man whose face looked familiar. Driving up closer, he recognized Molotov and offered him a lift home. As they were saying goodbye, the former Prime Minister said, 'My grandchildren will never believe that I was given a lift by Yuri Nikulin himself!'

But generally the Muscovites pass him in complete indifference. Members of the younger generation simply do not know who he is; after all, they have never seen his portrait in newspapers and magazines. Older people tell their friends, 'You know, I met Molotov yesterday. He's terribly old but still keeps going. And there was nobody guarding him.'

There have been encounters of another kind as well. A middle-aged woman once went up to Molotov in Pushkin Square and hurled abuse at him at the top of her voice, calling him a criminal and a murderer. Molotov did not say a word; he just hunched his shoulders and hurried away home. On another occasion Molotov joined a queue for tomatoes that had formed in a shop at Zhukovka. A woman immediately left the line and loudly announced that she would not stand in any line with an executioner. Molotov left the shop in silence. And Solzhenitsyn's wife, N. A. Reshetovskaya, ran into Molotov in the same shop when the Solzhenitsyns were staying at Rostropovich's dacha in Zhukovka. Solzhenitsyn asked her why she had said nothing to him. 'I would have gone up to him and said, "Are you Molotov? Well, I'm Solzhenitsyn. How can you go on living in this world with hands that have dripped blood?"'

At the opening of the play *The Steelworkers,* which was put on at the Moscow Arts Theatre, some members of the audience spotted Molotov and started asking him to autograph their programmes. For a moment he came to life. Then suddenly a young woman in the foyer began screaming, 'What are you doing? This man's an executioner! He destroyed hundreds of people!' The people around him scattered like autumn leaves. He lowered his head and quickly made for the exit. Another time, arriving home one winter in a taxi, he got out and, afraid of slipping, began to move cautiously towards the entrance of the house. Two burly men were coming towards him. One of them stopped, recognizing him, and said, 'What! You're not *still* creeping around, you vampire?'

Yes, Molotov is still with us. They say the good die young. Certainly, many of the others have been granted incredibly long lives.

5

L. M. Kaganovich:
Stalinist Commissar

Back in Moscow after twenty years spent in prisons and labour camps and after the Twentieth Party Congress, an old Bolshevik – let us call him D. – had arranged to visit a friend on the Frunze Embankment. Absent-mindedly he walked right past the entrance to his friend's building and entered instead the one next door. He went up in the lift and rang the doorbell of the apartment that he thought was his friend's. The door was opened by a very old man whom D. recognized instantly as Lazar Moiseyevich Kaganovich, formerly the leader of the Moscow Bolsheviks and an all-powerful Stalinist People's Commissar, the man whom D. regarded as directly responsible for the misfortunes he had suffered. D. was too surprised to utter a word, but Kaganovich, who did not recognize him, merely said, 'You must have made a mistake,' and closed the door. When D. told me the story he remarked with satisfaction, 'Kaganovich was expelled from the Party. Now I'm a member again – and Lazar was kicked out.' In D.'s view, justice had been done.

At one time Kaganovich enjoyed great popularity and wielded enormous power. The Lenin Metropolitan Underground Railway, which millions of Muscovites and visitors to the capital use every day, was known for more than twenty years as the Kaganovich Metro. His portrait used to be carried across Red Square on holidays; a place was always reserved for him on the tribune of the Lenin Mausoleum; his appearance in any auditorium was certain to prompt an ovation. Nowadays very few people recognize him. He once called out a doctor from the local health centre, and as the young woman spoke to the patient she addressed him several times as 'Citizen

Kazanovich'. 'Not Kazanovich – Kaganovich', he snapped irritably, adding, 'There was a time when my name was well known throughout the whole of the Soviet Union.'

Kaganovich is now 89 years old. He has survived his wife, his adopted son and all of his relatives except his daughter Maya, who is herself over 60 but calls on her father every day; he lives entirely alone. Devotedly Maya looks after a man on whose conscience there are quite as many crimes as there were on the consciences of those who were hanged in 1946 at Nuremberg under sentence of the International Tribunal.

Lazar Moiseyevich Kaganovich was born in November 1893, in a village called Kabana in the province of Kiev, one of a large number of children in a poor Jewish family. Too poor to complete his education, Lazar learned the craft of bootmaking and at the age of 14 began working in shoe factories and cobblers' workshops. Deprived of many of the rights that Russian and even other 'alien peoples' enjoyed, Jewish youth under the old regime was fertile soil for revolutionary agitation. It was recruited by all the oppositional parties – Zionists, Bundists, Anarchists, Socialist Revolutionaries, Mensheviks and those whom young Lazar chose to join in 1911, the Bolsheviks. His decision was influenced, no doubt, by his elder brother Mikhail, a metalworker who had himself become a Bolshevik in 1905. Two other Kaganovich brothers also became Bolsheviks.

The main task that Lazar Moiseyevich's party had set itself was to organize Bolshevik circles and groups in the leatherworking factories that were numerous in the Ukraine. Travelling from place to place, and occasionally experiencing brief arrests, Kaganovich established illegal circles and trade union groups of tanners and bootmakers in Kiev, Melitopol, Yekaterinoslav and elsewhere. Before the revolution he was working in a shoe factory in Yuzovka, where he also led a union of tanners and bootmakers. There he met the young N. S. Khrushchev, who, although not yet a member of the Bolshevik party, was also engaged in revolutionary work. Their association persisted, at least partly intact, well into later years.

In the spring of 1917 Kaganovich was called up and posted

for military training to the Forty-Second Infantry Regiment, which was stationed at Saratov. As a young soldier with seven years of illegal Party experience behind him as well as the gifts of an orator and agitator, he assumed a prominent place among the Saratov Bolsheviks and represented the garrison at an All-Russian conference of Bolshevik Army organizations. On his return to Saratov he was arrested but escaped and got himself illegally to Gomel, which was in the front-line zone. Within a few weeks he had become chairman of both the local bootmakers' and tanners' union and the Polessk Bolshevik Committee. The October Revolution found him in Gomel, where, under his leadership and without bloodshed, power passed into the hand of the soviets. Gomel was at that time a small provincial town, but it was also the railway junction for the front-line zone of the western front; if the Bolsheviks could control the railways of Belorussia, they would be in a position to oppose any movement of troops to put down the revolution in Petrograd.

During the revolution the Bolsheviks moved almost ceaselessly from one post to another, often in the most remote districts of the vast country. Kaganovich was elected a deputy to the Constituent Assembly on the Bolshevik list, and in December 1917 he was also appointed a delegate to the third All-Russian Congress of Soviets. With these two mandates he arrived in Petrograd. At the Congress of Soviets he was appointed to the All-Russian Executive Committee of the Russian Soviet Federative Socialist Republic (RSFSR) and stayed on to work in Petrograd. Together with the rest of the Executive Committee, he moved to Moscow in the spring of 1918. The civil war began, and for a time he worked as a Commissar for the 'organizational–agitational section of the All-Russian College for the Organization of the Workers' and Peasants' Red Army' – a whole host of organizations with such long names sprang up in those days. Soon he was sent to Nizhny-Novgorod, where he quickly progressed from agitator to chairman of the provincial Party committee as well as of the provincial soviet executive committee. During the heavy fighting against General Denikin in 1919, Kaganovich was ordered to the southern front, where he took part in eliminating a dangerous threat from the White Guard cavalry under K. K. Mamontov and A. G. Shkuro. Later, when the Red Army took Voronezh, he was appointed chairman of the revolutionary committee and the executive of the province of Voronezh.

In all probability Lenin knew little of Kaganovich. There is not a single letter or note by Lenin that mentions his name. Stalin and Molotov could not but know him, however, and they obviously singled him out among the local leaders. In the autumn of 1920 the Central Committee sent him to Central Asia, where he became a member of the Turkestan Commission of the All-Russian Central Executive Committee and the Council of People's Commissars and a member of the Central Asian Bureau of the Party Central Committee (the so-called 'Muslim Bureau'). At the same time he was People's Commissar of the Turkestan Workers' and Peasants' Inspectorate, a member of the Revolutionary Army Committee of the Turkestan Front and chairman of the Tashkent city soviet. He was also elected to the Central Executive Committee of the RSFSR. None of these appointments could have been made without Stalin's knowledge, as he was at that time both People's Commissar for Nationalities and of the Workers' and Peasants' Inspectorate for the RSFSR.

As soon as Stalin was appointed General Secretary of the Party's Central Committee in April 1922 he recalled Kaganovich from Central Asia and made him head of the section responsible for organizing – and soon also for posting – Party instructors. This was one of the most important jobs in the ever-expanding apparatus of the Central Committee, since it was Kaganovich's department that handled appointments to all responsible posts in the RSFSR and the USSR.

Stalin was a tough, harsh boss and demanded unquestioning, total subordination. Kaganovich was also stubborn and abrasive, but he never quarrelled with Stalin and immediately began to prove himself a wholly loyal worker, willing to carry out any assignment. It was a quality that Stalin appreciated, and Kaganovich soon became one of the most trusted members of Stalin's own 'shadow cabinet' – that is, the personal power structure that Stalin had begun to create inside the Party Central Committee even before Lenin died. Lazar Kaganovich quickly overtook his elder brother Mikhail, who in 1922 was district committee secretary in the small town of Vyksa and later head of the Economic Council of Nizhny-Novgorod province. In 1924, when he was only 30, Lazar Kaganovich was made both a member and a secretary of the Party Central Committee.

In the intense inner-Party struggle that developed after the death of Lenin, it was vital to Stalin to secure for himself the support of the Ukraine, which, after the RSFSR, was the most powerful Union republic. On Stalin's recommendation, it was Kaganovich who was appointed General Secretary of the Central Committee of the Communist Party of the Ukraine in 1925. The political situation in the republic at the time was very complex. The civil war had ended with a Bolshevik victory, but the peasant population still harboured strong nationalist and anarchist sentiments. The Bolshevik Party relied chiefly on the industrial regions with their predominantly Russian population, and it drew significant numbers of its members from among the Jews, who saw in Bolshevik authority a defence against the kind of oppression and pogroms that had swept the Jewish townships during the civil war. Ukrainian culture still lagged noticeably behind Russian culture and could not therefore constitute a serious obstacle to the Russification process that was already well advanced, as was demonstrated by the fact that Russian and Jewish youth accounted for more than half of all the students in institutions of higher learning in the Ukraine.

Two principles constituted the basis of state policy on the Ukraine. One, 'Ukrainianization', entailed the fostering of Ukrainian culture, the Ukrainian language and Ukrainian schools, the advancement of Ukrainians in the administrative apparatus and so on. The other was the urge to combat 'bourgeois and petty bourgeois nationalism'. Plainly, it would never be easy to draw a precise line between these two paths, especially in the towns and industrial centres, and Kaganovich showed that he inclined strongly towards the latter path and was ruthless in the face of anything that looked to him like Ukrainian nationalism. He had frequent clashes with V. Ya.

Chubar, the chairman of the Ukraine Economic Council, and
with A. Y. Shumsky, one of Kaganovich's most powerful
opponents, a member of the Ukraine Party Central Committee
and People's Commissar for Education in the Ukraine. In 1926
Shumsky managed to arrange an audience with Stalin and
insisted that Kaganovich be recalled. Although Stalin agreed
with some of Shumsky's arguments, he supported Kaganovich
and restricted himself to sending a special letter to the Politburo
of the Ukraine Communist Party.

Opposition to Kaganovich in the Ukraine grew. When
G. I. Petrovsky and Chubar came to Stalin with another
request for his recall, Stalin accused them of anti-Semitism, but
eventually, in 1928, he was nevertheless obliged to bring
Kaganovich back to Moscow. This transfer did not signify his
dissatisfaction with Kaganovich's performance, however, and
the latter once again became a secretary of the Party Central
Committee and a little later was also made a member of the
presidium of the Trade Unions Central Council, an appointment that was aimed at creating a counter-weight to the
leadership of M. P. Tomsky. At the beginning of 1930
Kaganovich became first secretary of the Moscow Party
committee and a fully-fledged member of the Politburo of the
All-Union Communist Party. He had arrived at the pinnacle of
Soviet – and his own – power.

In the summer of 1930, on the eve of the Sixteenth Party
Congress, the Moscow district Party conferences were held.
Lenin's widow, N. K. Krupskaya, spoke at the Bauman district
branch against the methods that Stalin was using in the
collectivization drive, declaring that this programme had
nothing in common with Lenin's co-operative scheme. She
accused the Party Central Committee of ignorance of the
peasants' mood and of refusing to consult the people. 'It is
pointless to blame the local organizations for all the mistakes
made by the Central Committee itself,' she declared.

While Krupskaya was making her speech, the district committee chiefs got word to Kaganovich, who came round to the
conference at once. He strode on to the platform when
Krupskaya had finished and subjected her speech to coarse and

scathing abuse. He repudiated her argument and added that as a
member of the Central Committee she had no right to utter her
criticism from the platform of a district Party conference.
'N. K. Krupskaya should not imagine', he declared, 'that she
has the monopoly on Leninism because she was Lenin's wife.'[1]

Although Stalin had rid the Politburo of the 'Right' –
Bukharin, Tomsky and Rykov – it was nonetheless not wholly
subservient to his will, and he sometimes found himself
opposed by S. M. Kirov, G. K. Ordzhonikidze, Ya. E.
Rudzutak, M. I. Kalinin and V. V. Kuybyshev. Kaganovich's
support could always be relied upon, however.

During collectivization, Stalin would always send Kaganovich to especially troublesome areas of the country, investing
him with full powers for the occasion. Kaganovich directed the
collectivization drive in the Ukraine, in the province of
Voronezh, in western Siberia and in many other areas. And
wherever he went his arrival signalled the widespread use of
force against the peasantry, the deportation of not only tens of
thousands of kulaks but also many thousands of so-called
'kulak's men' and their families – which meant in practice
anyone who resisted collectivization. Kaganovich applied especially cruel force against the peasant Cossack population of the
Northern Caucasus. It is enough to recall that under pressure
from Kaganovich the Northern Caucasus bureau of the Party
area committee took the decision in the autumn of 1932 to
deport to the north the population of sixteen major Cossack
villages. (An average Cossack village was considerably larger
than a Russian one, and each would have had a population of
not less than a thousand households.) Simultaneously, peasants
from the non-black-earth region, where there was less arable
land at the disposal of the villages, were transported to the
Northern Caucasus and settled in the places thus 'liberated'.
Harsh repression was carried out in the Moscow areas that were
under Kaganovich's administration and at that time covered the
territory of several of the regions of today.

It was no doubt Stalin's appreciation of this 'agrarian
experience' that led him to appoint Kaganovich head of the
newly created agricultural section of the Party Central Committee. In 1933–34 Kaganovich ran the political sections of the

Machine-Tractor Stations and state farms, which for a time dominated all the organs of Soviet power in the agrarian sector, including, to some extent, the purge of the 'kulak's men' and 'saboteurs' on the collective farms.

Workers as well as peasants learned to fear Kaganovich's uncompromising authority. In Ivanovo-Voznesensk men and women went on strike in 1932 over the appalling shortage of food, and it was Kaganovich who supervised the punishment of the strike leaders. Then some of the local officials boycotted the special 'closed' shops that had recently been introduced for Party workers and sent their wives and children to stand in line at the ordinary food shops like everyone else. Kaganovich regarded this behaviour as an 'anti-Party deviation' and reprimanded them severely.

Kaganovich was Stalin's right-hand man at this stage. During 1932–34 letters would come from all over the country addressed to 'Comrades I. V. Stalin and L. M. Kaganovich'. Because many institutions in Moscow were involved in cultural and ideological affairs, Kaganovich was assigned to deal with ideological issues. In 1932, for example, a commission under his chairmanship banned the staging of N. R. Erdman's play *The Suicide* (which was recently put on in Moscow, fifty years after it was originally banned and many years after the author had died). He had to cope with questions of foreign policy as well. Foreign policy decisions were made not in the Council of People's Commissars but in the Politburo, as former Foreign Commissariat assistant E. A. Gnedin confirms:

> The Foreign Commissariat apparatus was aware that there was a Politburo commission of non-permanent members that was responsible for foreign policy. I happened to attend one of its night-time sessions in the early 1930s. Directives were given concerning an important leading article that I had to write for *Izvestiya* on the subject of foreign policy. The chief editor of *Pravda,* L. Z. Mekhlis, was there too. Other matters were discussed first. The decisions were made by Molotov and Kaganovich, the latter acting as chairman. Deputy Commissars M. N. Krestinky and B. S. Stomonyakov gave reports, and I was amazed that these two important figures, both experts on the topics under discussion, should be here in the position of

applicants. Their submissions – they could hardly be called
reports – were summarily either agreed or rejected. It is worth
noting that Kaganovich responded with sarcasm even to
Molotov's remarks.[2]

During this period Kaganovich also had the job of running
the Central Committee Transport Commission, and when
Stalin was away for his Black Sea holidays it was he who would
take over in Moscow as deputy boss of the Party. He was one of
the very first people to be awarded the country's highest mark
of distinction, the Order of Lenin, when it was introduced.

As early as the 1920s an important weapon in the consolida-
tion of Stalin's power was the Party purge – that is, the periodic
check of the entire Party membership and the mass expulsion of
the unworthy and the incompetent. When regular, systematic
purges were instituted in 1933 it was Kaganovich who was
appointed chairman of the Party Control Commission under
the Central Committee. Apart from Stalin himself, nobody else
in the entire country at that time held as many key posts in the
Party power structure as Kaganovich. It was he who, as
chairman of the Organizing Committee for the Seventeenth
Party Congress, falsified the results of the secret ballot in the
Central Committee, destroying some 300 voting slips on which
Stalin's name had been crossed out.

A. E. Kolman, who worked in the scientific department of
the Moscow city committee of the Party in the mid-1930s,
recalls in his memoirs that he frequently saw Kaganovich and
Khrushchev at close quarters, since as Central Committee
secretaries they were responsible, one after the other, for
supervising his department, and he had to report to them daily.
He also saw them frequently at sessions of the Secretariat and of
his bureau:

I remember them both very well. They both bubbled with
vitality and energy, and, different from each other as they may
have been, they were also a lot alike. Kaganovich in particular
possessed a superhuman capacity for work. They both compen-
sated (not always successfully) for their lack of education and
general culture by intuition, improvization, native wit and great

natural gifts. Kaganovich had a bent for systematizing and even theorizing the work, while Khrushchev's penchant was for pragmatism and technique. . . .

Before they were corrupted by power they were both very easy-going, straightforward, slap-on-the-back types, open-hearted in the 'Russian style', especially Khrushchev, who was not ashamed to learn from his inferiors and would ask me to explain scientific subtleties that he could not understand. Kaganovich was more reserved than Khrushchev; he never permitted himself the shouting and foul language that earned him his reputation later on when he was imitating Stalin – or so it was alleged.[3]

This image of Kaganovich in the mid-1930s is somewhat embellished. His behaviour with the lower ranks was not what it was with executives in the city and provincial Party committees, and especially in the Central Committee Secretariat and bureau. He showed how ruthless he could be clearly enough during collectivization, as we have seen. The old Bolshevik I. P. Aleksakhin remembers his arrival in the Yefremov District (then in Moscow oblast) in 1933, when there were problems with the state grain procurements. The first thing Kaganovich did was to take the Party membership card away from Utkin, the chairman of the district executive committee, who was also secretary of the district Party committee, with the warning that if the grain-procurement quota was not met within three days, Utkin would be expelled from the Party, relieved of his job and imprisoned. Utkin reasoned that the grain-procurement quota had been assessed on the basis of the standing crop in May, whereas only half the quantity of grain and potatoes had been realized at the harvest. To this Kaganovich responded in the language of the gutter and accused Utkin of right-wing opportunism. Despite the fact that Moscow committee representatives (like I. P. Aleksakhin) worked in the villages until well into the autumn, and although they took even food grain, potatoes and seeds from the peasants and kolkhozes, only 68 per cent of the procurement quota was met. Utkin was expelled from the Party. Nearly half the local population left the district after that 'procurement' campaign, first destroying their huts.

The local agricultural economy was devastated, and for three years grain and potatoes had to be imported into the district.

Of course, Kaganovich's transformation took some time, but under Stalin's influence and given the corrupting effects of unlimited power he gradually became coarser and harsher. Moreover, as he was afraid of becoming a victim himself of the savage times in which he was living, he took refuge in destroying the lives of others. Naturally, in Moscow he did not conduct himself as he behaved in the rural districts of Yefremov; but even at the Moscow city committee meetings he grew ruder and more and more ill-mannered. If he grovelled to Stalin, Kaganovich was known to be tyrannical when dealing with his own subordinates. An assistant or secretary who brought him a file of letters for signing might well have it thrown in his or her face, and there were even occasions when he resorted to physical violence.

Kaganovich grew increasingly hostile to the advancement in 1934–35 of N. I. Yezhov, who was becoming Stalin's favourite and was pushing Kaganovich out of some of his positions in the Party apparatus. He also had unfriendly relations with the young Malenkov, who was progressing very quickly at the heart of the Central Committee machine. These and other conflicts pleased Stalin greatly, and as always he skilfully fanned the enmity between his closest assistants.

From the early 1930s onwards the radical reconstruction of Moscow began. As the helmsman of the Moscow Bolsheviks, Kaganovich was one of the organizers of the work, resolving single-handedly many of the problems that arose, though he discussed the most important of them with Stalin and the Politburo. Moscow was, of course, much in need of rebuilding, and the general direction of the reconstruction was properly planned to preserve the historical outlines of the old city highways and streets. Nevertheless, from the start little care was taken to preserve the most valuable monuments of Russia's capital. The great church of Christ the Saviour was demolished to make way for the planned Palace of Soviets. Where the Holy Week monastery once stood you will now find the Russia

Cinema. With Kaganovich's knowledge, and often on his initiative, dozens of Moscow's churches were demolished, despite the fact that they in no way hampered the city's reconstruction and were, indeed, vital elements in its historic architectural heritage. The Iversk Gates and clocktower near Red Square, and the church on the corner of Nikolskaya Street (now 25 October Street) were torn down in the face of outspoken protest from A. V. Lunacharsky, People's Commissar for Education, and leading architects. (In his summing up of a discussion with them, Kaganovich stated categorically . . . 'And *my* aesthetics demands that the demonstration processions from the six districts of Moscow should all pour into Red Square at the same time.') The famous Sukharev Tower was demolished. (A number of architects are now trying to get it reconstructed, using plans that have been preserved.) A great part of the Kitay-Gorod wall was destroyed, and even within the Kremlin itself several churches dating from the fifteenth to the seventeenth centuries were demolished.

To be sure, Kaganovich's activities were not restricted to the destruction of ancient monuments. A great deal of construction was also going on in the Moscow of the mid-1930s. One of the main achievements connected with the name of Kaganovich was the building of the Moscow Metropolitan Underground Railway, which was formerly named after him, as I have mentioned. A former reporter for the *Vechernyaya Moskva* (*Evening Moscow*) newspaper, A. V. Khrabrovitsky, recalls:

He looked into all the details of the planning and building work; he climbed down into the shafts and foundations and forced his way, doubled over, along damp tunnels, chatting with the workers. I remember a site meeting that he held in a tunnel under Dzerzhinsky Square, where they were having difficulty in sinking the shaft. He had apparently been to Berlin, incognito, in order to study the Metro there, and when he got back, he reported that the entrances to the Berlin Metro were mere holes in the ground, whereas we were going to have beautiful pavilions.

It was Kaganovich's wish that the first line of the Metro should be completed by the seventeenth anniversary of the October Revolution, 7 November 1934, 'whatever it takes to do it'. I can recall his words. On 24 March, at the all-Moscow *subbotnik* – instead of taking their day off, citizens would voluntarily give a day's work unpaid – Kaganovich, hard at work with a shovel, was asked for his impressions. He replied, 'I will form my impressions on 7 November.' The poet A. I. Bezymensky wrote:

> The Metro you are building,
> Fired by Stalin's strength,
> Lazar Kaganovich will launch
> On November Seventh.

However, after the shafts had been inspected in April of that year by Molotov, Khrushchev and Bulganin – in Kaganovich's absence – the timetable was altered, as there were signs that the work was of poor quality because of the rushed schedule and that some unpleasantness could lie ahead. The press stopped writing about the launch dates. . . .

I always saw Khrushchev together with Kaganovich. Kaganovich was the active, the powerful one, whereas all I ever heard Khrushchev saying was, 'Yes, Lazar Moiseyevich', 'Right, Lazar Moiseyevich'. . . .[4]

The first line of the Metro was launched in mid-May 1935.

While the work on the Metro and the old city was going on, a general plan was being feverishly assembled for the transformation of Moscow as the capital of the country. Hundreds of architects and builders and all kinds of specialists were allocated to the task, which was also under Kaganovich's direction. A. E. Kolman later recalled:

In 1933 or 1934 Kaganovich invited me, as a mathematician, to take part in the commission he was heading to form a plan for the reconstruction of Moscow. The job of the commission was to finalize the plan which hundreds of specialists had already been working on for a long time: our task was to convert a vast pile of materials into a compact document for the Politburo to approve. We worked literally day and night, usually till three in the morning and sometimes until dawn – that was the usual style of working in those years, and right up to Stalin's death, in all Party, soviet and other institutions. The working capacity of our commission and its chairman was unbelievable. During the final stages of the work, Kaganovich sent five of us to stay at a dacha at the disposal of the city committee, where, undisturbed by the sound of telephones, we were able to finish off the work quickly and to present the completed plan to the Politburo.

We were invited to the Politburo session at which the plan was discussed. The Politburo members and Central Committee secretaries sat at a long, T-shaped table in a huge, oblong room, while we, the members of the commission, sat on chairs along the wall. At the centre of the short side of the T Stalin sat alone in state, with his assistant, Poskrebyshev, at one side. In fact, that was only where Stalin's place was laid; he spent his time pacing back and forth along each side of the table during and after the report, puffing on his short pipe and casting an occasional sidelong look at the people around the table. Of us he took not the slightest notice. Since the plan had been circulated before the meeting, Kaganovich gave only the most condensed outline of its chief proposals and mentioned the enormous amount of work done by the commission. Stalin then asked for questions, but there were none. Apparently, they all understood perfectly well what to us, who had worked on the project for months, were enormously complicated problems and far from clear. 'Does anyone wish to say anything?' Stalin asked. There was silence. Stalin went on pacing up and down, and it seemed to me that he was smirking behind his moustache. Finally, he went over to the table, picked up the red file of plan proposals, leafed through it and then asked Kaganovich, 'I see that the proposal is to get rid of all the basements in Moscow: how many are there?' We had come fully prepared, of course, and one of his assistants immediately leaped to Kaganovich's side and handed him the figure he wanted, which turned out to be very considerable, as thousands of apartments and other forms of accommodation were tucked away under the city's pavements.

On hearing the figures, Stalin took his pipe out of his mouth and spoke. 'The proposal to eliminate the basements is demagoguery. As for the rest of the plan, it should be approved. What do you think, comrades?' Everyone made short speeches of approval, and the plan was passed with minor amendments. Closing the discussion, Kaganovich apologized for the basements, saying that it had been included by mistake. It was a clumsy evasion. We all knew that before signing such an important document he would have read it several times over.[5]

On moving to a new job in 1935, Kaganovich handed over control of the Moscow city and oblast Party organization to N. S. Khrushchev. It was Kaganovich himself who had advanced Khrushchev, at first appointing him to run the Bauman and Krasnaya Presnya Party district committees and then promoting him to be his own deputy in the Moscow organization.

Kaganovich was a leading figure in the appalling purge of the Party and the whole of society that swept in waves over the USSR from 1936 to 1938. It was he who conducted the terror among the Commissariats of Railways and Heavy Industry in Moscow (in fact, throughout the railway network and in heavy industrial enterprises) and against the managers of the Metro-building programme. During the investigations that were carried out after the Twentieth Party Congress of 1956 dozens of letters from Kaganovich to the NKVD were discovered, complete with lists 'of the Party workers whom he wanted arrested. In many cases he personally checked draft verdicts and made arbitrary alterations. He knew what he was doing. Stalin placed so much faith in him at that period that the leader even made him privy to his plan of staging a 'great purge' as early as 1935. Not surprisingly, therefore, it was Kaganovich who was dispatched to a number of regions of the country charged with the task of implementing this 'great purge'. He carried out repressions in Chelyabinsk, Yaroslav and Ivanovo oblasts and in the Donbas. He had barely arrived in Ivanovo when he sent a cable to Stalin, which read: 'First sight of materials proves necessity for immediate arrest obkom secretary D. S. Yepanchikov. Also necessary arrest obkom propaganda manager M. E. Mikhailov.'

Having armed himself with Stalin's sanction, Kaganovich proceeded with the wholesale destruction of the Ivanovo oblast Party committee. At the beginning of August 1937, speaking at the much reduced plenum of the committee, he accused the Party organization of conniving with 'enemies of the people'. The plenum itself took place in an atmosphere of terror and intimidation. For example, the secretary of the Ivanovo city committee, A. A. Vasiliev, had only to voice some doubt about the 'hostile activities' of the arrested obkom employees for Kaganovich to cut him short abruptly and for Vasiliev to be expelled from the Party then and there and, shortly after, to be arrested as an 'enemy of the people'. The same fate overtook the chairman of the Ivanovo oblast trade union council, I. N. Simagin, a member of the Party since 1905.[6]

Kaganovich arrived in the Donbas in 1937 to carry out a similar purge and behaved there with the same boorishness and cruelty. He immediately called a meeting of the local Party people who were concerned with the economy. In a report entitled 'On Sabotage' he declared that right there in the hall, sitting among the local leadership, were not a few 'enemies of the people' and 'saboteurs'; and that very night the NKVD arrested about 140 prominent Donbas people, factory and mine managers, chief engineers and Party leaders. The lists of those to be arrested had been approved the evening before by Kaganovich.

One sometimes hears the claim that Kaganovich's two younger brothers perished in the years of the great terror. This is not true. Yuli was first secretary of the Gorky (formerly Nizhny-Novgorod) provincial and city committees of the Party in the mid-1930s. He was soon released and transferred to Moscow to work in the People's Commissariat of Foreign Trade, where he was made a member of the board. In the 1940s he was the Soviet trade delegate to Mongolia. At the beginning of the 1950s he died after a long illness.

The younger brother was the manager of the main department store in Kiev and later head of the city department of trade. He never rose to the higher levels of power, and, according to people who were close to the family, he was never a victim of the repressions. Only a Kaganovich cousin suffered in the 1930s. As for Mikhail, he was appointed People's Commissar of Defence Industries in 1937.

From the middle of the 1930s onwards Stalin involved Kaganovich, then second in importance in the Party machine, in the administration of the country's economy. The transport system in particular was proving to be a major bottleneck, but as Transport Commissar Kaganovich soon effected a noticeable improvement by applying certain well tried methods – threats and terror. The number of accidents was reduced, and the trains began to run on time. At the end of 1937 he was made Commissar for Heavy Industry; in early 1939 he became Commissar for Fuel Production and deputy chairman of the Council of People's Commissars under Molotov.

Not surprisingly, the Soviet press constantly acclaimed him 'Stalin's Commissar' and chief trouble-shooter. Articles and features appeared in newspapers and magazines commending Kaganovich's humanity and his concern for the common man. Regrettably, the campaign was joined even by A. P. Platonov, an outstanding writer. After reading Platonov's *The Foundation Ditch* and *Chevengur,* Stalin declared, 'He's a talented writer, but a swine'; Platonov, disgraced and hitherto unable to get his work accepted by magazines and publishing houses, managed at the end of 1936 to publish a short story called *Immortality,* which was nothing other than a tawdry boot-licking exercise. The central episode of the story is an unexpected telephone call at dawn from Kaganovich to Levin, the station master of a remote halt called Red Stage:

'How did you get to the phone so quickly?' the People's Commissar asked. 'When did you manage to get dressed? Weren't you asleep?' (Levin had not yet gone to bed). 'People go to bed at night, not in the morning. Listen, Emmanuel Semyonovich, if you will put your backs into it at Red Stage, I'll answer for the wear and tear on a thousand locos. I'll check to see when you're asleep, but don't make me your nanny.'

'It must be night-time in Moscow, too, Lazar Moiseyevich,' Levin said quietly.

Kaganovich understood and laughed. The People's Commissar asked how he might help. 'You already have, Lazar Moiseyevich.'

The next evening Levin gets home at midnight – 'He got into bed and tried hard to fall asleep quickly, not for the pleasure of rest but for the next day's work' – but an hour later he is woken by the telephone. The watchman on guard at the station tells him that Kaganovich has just rung up from Moscow to ask how Levin is and whether or not he is asleep. Levin cannot sleep now. He sits for a while, then dresses and goes to the station, thinking about how to increase the loading norms of the wagons.[7]

The war years were a difficult time for all the Soviet leadership, Kaganovich included. The railways, which even in normal conditions were overloaded, now had to handle an enormous volume of military equipment and personnel and the evacuation of thousands of enterprises to the east of the country; responsibility for their smooth running fell directly on Kaganovich's shoulders. He was not at first a member of the State Defence Committee but was soon appointed to it, together with N. A. Bulganin, Mikoyan and N. A. Voznesensky. The fact that the railways managed to cope with their huge burden was without doubt to Kaganovich's credit and earned him, in September 1943, the title of Hero of Socialist Labour.

While continuing to discharge his primary duties in Moscow, in 1942–43 Kaganovich was also a member of the Northern Caucasus War Council, though his visits to the front were generally brief. When the Germans broke through in the south in 1942 and began to advance towards the Caucasus and the Volga, he flew to the front charged with the special task of organizing the work of the military tribunals and prosecutors. In those months many Red Army commanders and commissars paid with their lives for failures and mistakes that should have been blamed on the high command.

By 1944 Kaganovich was becoming more and more involved in economic work, with post-war problems in view. He remained deputy chairman of the Council of People's Commissars – they would be called Ministers after 1946 – and took over the building materials industry, one of the most backward sectors of the economy.

By the end of the war Kaganovich's influence over the leadership of both the Party and the country was on the wane. He was still given important jobs, but the policy for the war economy, laid down by the Council of People's Commissars and the State Defence Committee, was under the general direction of N. A. Voznesensky, while Party policy was handled by G. M. Malenkov. Voznesensky frequently chaired sessions of the Council of People's Commissars in the years 1945–46, and by 1946 Kaganovich ranked only ninth in the Party hierarchy, after Stalin, Molotov, Beria, Zhdanov, Malenkov, Voznesensky, Kalinin and Voroshilov.

In 1947 he was made First Secretary of the Communist Party of the Ukraine. Because of a severe drought the republic had failed to meet its grain-procurement target, and Stalin was dissatisfied with Khrushchev, who had been running the Party there for some nine years. The move obviously represented demotion for Kaganovich, and he worked with none of his customary energy. Moreover, Khrushchev was not moved from his previous job but remained chairman of the Ukraine Council of Ministers – no longer the Khrushchev of Moscow of the 1930s, with his 'Yes, Lazar Moiseyevich', 'Right, Lazar Moiseyevich' – and clashes between the two men were frequent. Kaganovich devoted little of his time to agriculture, preferring instead to rekindle the embers of the old fight against 'nationalism', transferring personnel (and often removing the best and most valuable people from their posts). He sent frequent memoranda to Stalin, without first showing them to Khrushchev, even though he had no special powers during this second period of office in the Ukraine. Stalin, however, demanded that such communications also be signed by Khrushchev, a clear indication that he no longer trusted Kaganovich. Then in 1947, when there was an excellent harvest that clearly owed more to the spring rains than to the efforts of Kaganovich, it was obvious that he was doing no good there. Khrushchev had far greater influence in the Ukraine, whereas Kaganovich had earned little credit in the republic after his efforts there in the 1920s. He returned to Moscow at the end of 1947 and resumed his work in the Council of Ministers of the USSR, as the Council of People's Commissars was now called.

His position in Moscow grew more and more difficult, however. The notorious campaign against 'rootless cosmopolitans', which aimed at undermining ideological and cultural activists of Jewish nationality, was gathering force. The Party and state machines were purged of Jews; they were not admitted to the diplomatic or security services, and their entry was curtailed to any institutes that prepared personnel for the defence industries and the most important branches of science. They were no longer admitted to military academies or Party schools, and there were wholesale arrests of Jewish intellectuals.

Kaganovich cannot be blamed for initiating these arrests, but neither did he protest against them or come out in defence of a single person. Joseph Berger recalls that a fellow camp inmate was a close relative of Kaganovich:

> He was arrested in 1949, and his wife attempted to get an audience with Kaganovich. It was nine months before he would see her, and then, even before she opened her mouth, he said, 'You surely don't imagine that if I could have done anything, I would have waited nine months? You must understand: there is only one Sun; the rest are all pathetic little planets.'[8]

Kaganovich himself frequently behaved like an anti-Semite at that time and was irritated by the presence of Jews in his own apparatus and among his 'retainers'. He could be astonishingly petty. One example will serve. The screening of foreign films was often arranged for Politburo members at state dachas, and a translator was always present to interpret the dialogue. On one occasion, at Kaganovich's dacha, the translator was a Jewish girl who knew Italian perfectly but spoke Russian with a very strong Jewish accent. Kaganovich gave instructions that she was never to come again.

One victim of the spy mania of the years after the war was Kaganovich's elder brother, Mikhail, who had been removed in 1940 from his post as People's Commissar for Aircraft Production and, at the Eighteenth Party Conference in the spring of 1941, from the Party Central Committee. He was slanderously accused of sabotage in the aviation industry and even of secret collaboration with the Nazis. The Politburo investigated these ludicrous charges; Beria submitted the report, and Kaganovich said nothing in his brother's defence. Stalin praised Lazar Moiseyevich disingenuously for not letting family feeling stand in the way of his 'principles' and, with equal hypocrisy, suggested that they should not rush to arrest Mikhail Moiseyevich but should set up a commission, headed by

Mikoyan, to examine the charges that had been brought against him. A few days later Mikhail Kaganovich was invited to Mikoyan's office. Beria came too, accompanied by the man who had given evidence against Mikhail and who was now made to repeat his accusations. 'This man is insane,' Mikhail said, but he knew perfectly well what this little scene meant for him. He asked Mikoyan if there was a lavatory that he could use, and Mikoyan indicated a door. Mikhail, who had a revolver in his pocket, left the room. A few seconds later a loud shot rang out. He was buried without publicity.

Kaganovich saw Stalin less and less and was no longer invited to the dinners that the leader gave. At the Nineteenth Party Congress in 1952 he was included in the enlarged Presidium of the Central Committee – which replaced the Politburo until 1966, when it was restored by Brezhnev – and even in the Bureau of the Central Committee, but he was not one of the group of Stalin's five most trusted Party leaders.

Another widespread anti-Semitic campaign was launched with the famous 'Doctors' Plot', the arrest of the Kremlin doctors, most of them Jews, who were charged with sabotage and espionage. Some books published in the West, notably A. Avtorkhanov's *Zagadka smerti Stalina* (*The Mystery of Stalin's Death*), contain numerous inventions and contradictions, including the assertion that Kaganovich protested loudly against the persecution of the Jews in the Soviet Union and that he issued an ultimatum to Stalin demanding the re-examination of the 'Doctors' Affair'. Kaganovich, moreover, allegedly 'tore up his membership card of the Presidium of the Party Central Committee and threw the pieces in Stalin's face. Stalin was about to call the Kremlin guard when he had a stroke and fell to the floor unconscious.'[9]

Avtorkhanov cites the writer Ilya Ehrenburg as his source, but on the many occasions that I met Ehrenburg between 1964 and 1966, when we often spoke about Stalin, he never recounted anything that accords even remotely with Avtorkhanov's reported evidence, nor could he possibly have known anything about the circumstances of Stalin's death. The whole account is pure invention. Kaganovich was anyway quite incapable of rebelling against Stalin. At the beginning of 1953 he was lying low, watching the course of events in fear and trembling. It was Stalin's death that saved Kaganovich, like many others, and not only Jews.

With Stalin's death Kaganovich's influence waxed again, if only briefly. He became a member of the new, smaller Party Presidium and headed several important Ministries in his capacity as one of the first deputy chairmen of the Council of Ministers. He supported Khrushchev and Malenkov in their plot to arrest and eliminate Beria. Earlier he had supported all the steps that were taken to review the 'Doctors' Affair' and to put an end to the anti-Semitic campaign. Even his brother Mikhail was posthumously rehabilitated.

However, for Kaganovich life became if anything more complicated when the first rehabilitations started in 1953–54, since not all the victims of the terror had been shot or had died in the camps. People began to return to Moscow who knew perfectly well that Kaganovich had played a leading part in the implementation of the mass terror. For instance, by 1954 A. V. Snegov, who had known Kaganovich when he was engaged in Party work in the Ukraine in the 1920s, was fully rehabilitated; at Khrushchev's suggestion, he was given a job in the political section of the Ministry of Internal Affairs. In the interval at a ceremonial meeting in the Bolshoy Theatre, on the occasion of the thirty-eighth anniversary of the October Revolution, Kaganovich suddenly spotted Snegov walking arm-in-arm with G. I. Petrovsky, who was then still running the Museum of the Revolution. Kaganovich hurried over to them with his hand outstretched. Snegov ignored it. 'I will not shake a hand that is stained with the blood of the Party's best people,' he said in a voice loud enough to be heard by all around them. Kaganovich's face darkened, and he moved away quickly with his daughter. But by then he had no power to punish or persecute his enemies.

He protested vigorously against Khrushchev's intention to expose Stalin's crimes to the delegates at the Twentieth Party Congress in 1956. When it was suggested that an opportunity to speak at the Congress be given to old Bolsheviks who had returned from the camps, Kaganovich exclaimed, 'And are these ex-convicts to judge us?' But even Kaganovich had to say something in his speech to the Congress, albeit in passing, about the harm done by the cult of personality. In the event Khrushchev overcame all opposition, and at the end of the Congress he read his famous 'secret' speech.

Kaganovich's relations with Molotov and Malenkov had been bad in the past, but now the three of them collaborated, prompted by their general hostility to Khrushchev and his policies. With great thoroughness they recorded his every mistake in the management of industry and agriculture, although what they hated most was his 'destalinization' policy and the release and rehabilitation of millions of political prisoners. The anti-Khrushchev group's venture ended in defeat, however. Molotov, Malenkov, Kaganovich (and Shepilov 'because of his association with them') were drummed out of the Politburo, and their names and their scheme were discussed and condemned at all Party meetings – they were the Soviet Union's 'Gang of Four'.

After the June Plenum Kaganovich was terrified. He expected to be arrested at any moment and to suffer the same fate as Beria. After all, the crimes on his conscience were hardly less grave than Beria's. He even went so far as to telephone Khrushchev and beg humbly to be treated with clemency. He reminded Khrushchev of their old friendship, of the fact that it had been he, Kaganovich, who had helped Khrushchev to advance so quickly in the Moscow Party organization. Khrushchev told him that there would be no reprisals as long as the anti-Party group abandoned their struggle against the Party line and worked in good faith at the jobs that the Party would now give them. In fact, Kaganovich was soon sent to Solikamsk, in Perm oblast, as manager of the Urals Potash Works, the largest of its kind in the country.

In 1933, during a Party purge, all responsible Party workers had had to appear before a purge commission. Khrushchev underwent his purge in the Party organization of the Moscow Aviakhim (Aerochemical) plant. He was asked in particular how he applied the principle of socialist competition in his work, and he replied, 'Who am I to compete with? There's only Lazar Moiseyevich, and surely I can't compete with him?' In the

1930s Khrushchev could not 'compete' with Kaganovich, of course, but in the 1940s the clashes between them were frequent, and in the second half of the 1950s Khrushchev inflicted a decisive political defeat on the Politburo group that included Kaganovich. His dominance was now complete.

At the Twenty-Second Party Congress of October 1961 Khrushchev again raised the question of Stalin's crimes and those of his closest aides, and he returned to the subject of the 'anti-Party group' of Molotov, Malenkov and Kaganovich. Many of the delegates cited Kaganovich's crimes and produced documents and facts that demonstrated his active participation in the terror. His expulsion from the Party was demanded by a number of delegates.

Kaganovich worked in Solikamsk until the end of 1961. Having been distinguished in all his previous jobs by his harsh treatment of subordinates, in Solikamsk he was in all respects the model of a fair-minded boss. Nevertheless, soon after the Congress he was removed from his post as manager of the potash works and, on his return to Moscow, was expelled from the Party by the bureau of his local branch in the Krasnaya Presnya district. (When Khrushchev was removed from his posts in 1964 Kaganovich requested the Central Committee to restore his own Party membership, but the Presidium declined to review its previous decision.)

The post in Solikamsk was his last. At 67 years old he returned to Moscow to begin as an ordinary old-age pensioner on the 120 roubles a month that is the maximum pension for all civilians. It was not very much, but Stalin's former Commissar had put aside quite enough to ensure a comfortable life for himself. Even so, he once telephoned P. N. Pospelov, the director of the Marxism–Leninism Institute, and, complaining of his small pension, asked to be sent free of charge the Institute's journal, *Voprosy istorii KPSS* (*Questions of Party History*), which, like all Party journals, cost very little, a mere 40 kopeks.

Without any difficulty he registered as a reader at the History Library, entering on the application form 'higher' as the level of education that he had achieved. Sometimes he also went to the Lenin Library, where he started to write his memoirs, judging by the books and journals that the librarians helped him choose – on events in Saratov and Gomel in 1917, Turkestan affairs in 1920–22, Party organizational work in the 1920s, the history of the Moscow Party organization. He often sat and read the newspapers in the Library too, taking no notice of the many visitors who eyed him with curiosity.

Each year he received permission to stay at an ordinary rest home, where he would mix with the other holidaymakers and where middle-aged workers would gladly pass the time in his company, since he was a practised agitator who knew how to talk and an ex-worker with a wealth of experience. He never touched on the subject of the Stalin terror or his part in it. He also liked to travel on the Moscow river-bus; when the price of the tickets increased he grumbled that when he had run Moscow's transport system such things never happened.

Of course, there were some unpleasant moments for Kaganovich as well. For example, he was once spotted on the street by a group of men who happened to be the sons of Party workers who had perished in the Ukraine during the terror. Some of them, including the son of V. Ya. Chubar, had spent years in the labour camps themselves. Immediately they surrounded Kaganovich and cursed him as a hangman and scoundrel. He was very frightened and shouted for help: 'Guards! They're killing me! Militia!' The militia duly appeared, rounded up the men and took them to the nearest militia post, where the affair was briskly dispatched – they all gave their names and were immediately released.

One day in the early 1970s the famous actress Alissa Koonen, then over 80, was visiting the grave of her husband A. Ya. Tairov, in the Novo-Devichy Cemetery. Tairov had been the irreplaceable director of the Kamerny (Chamber) Theatre, which he directed from 1914 to 1946, when he was dismissed, though he returned to produce plays there until 1949. As early as 1929, in a letter to the playwright V. M. Bil-Belotserkovsky, Stalin described Tairov's theatre as 'bourgeois'. At that time such a statement was of no significance, but when in 1949 this letter was included in Stalin's

Collected Works the ever-popular Kamerny Theatre was accused of formalism and closed down. Tairov died the following year.

As she was standing at his graveside, his widow was approached by an old man who told her how much he admired her for the many roles that he remembered seeing her play. 'Excuse me,' the actress interrupted, 'but to whom am I speaking?'

'I am Lazar Moiseyevich Kaganovich', the old man replied. 'Tell me, Alissa Georgiyevna, after what happened to Tairov and to you, did your friends abandon you?'

'No, why should they?' the actress answered. 'When they closed down our theatre I couldn't meet my fans outside the stage door after performances, of course, but we had many friends and relations, and they always stuck by us.'

'Yes,' Kaganovich mused, 'your world is very different from ours.'

Alissa Koonen said nothing, bowed coldly and left. She told her friends later that Kaganovich had expressed his admiration for her work and added: 'Yet one word from him in 1949 could have saved our theatre.'

Kaganovich had always enjoyed good health and had scarcely ever needed medical treatment. Age began to tell, however, and in 1980 he was admitted to a urological hospital, where he was assigned to a ward with twenty other beds. Dozens of patients from all over the hospital came to have a look at the former leader; since most of the patients were elderly, they remembered Kaganovich only too well. The senior physician had to install him in his own office and hang a large curtain over the glass door. Even the hospital staff took sides. In the evenings the older nurses quarrelled with each other over how many lumps of sugar to put in his tea: 'You've given him four again! Two's enough for that old bugger! Let him have the same as everyone else!' His daughter overcame her timidity and wrote to the Central Committee with a request that her father be given some relief. She received an unexpected telephone call from the Party administration and was told that in future Kaganovich would receive treatment at the Kremlin hospital and that his 'Kremlin rations' would be restored to him. He was pleased by the news, but he could not refrain from muttering,

'I'd rather have back my red card' (that is, his Party membership card).

To relieve the boredom of isolation, Kaganovich would often spend some time in the large yard outside his apartment house and indulge in a game of dominoes with other old men. In fact, he was soon the acknowledged dominoes champion of the neighbourhood. Play would normally come to an end when daylight failed until Kaganovich, calling on the services of some of his old contacts, somehow persuaded the local authorities to provide a shelter with electric light. Now the old-age pensioners of the Frunze Embankment can play dominoes until late at night.

Not long ago Kaganovich suffered a stroke, but his strong constitution has survived even that – and anyway the treatment in the Kremlin clinic is considerably better than that offered by an ordinary hospital. He will soon be up and about again, taking walks in the quiet lanes off the Frunze Embankment and playing dominoes with the other pensioners. Kaganovich, Stalin's closest comrade-in-arms for twenty-five years, who strained every nerve to help the despot to run his fearful machine of terror, is living out his time quietly in the back streets of Moscow.

6

G. M. Malenkov: the 'Heir' that Never Was

Not long ago I was visiting a friend at the hospital for old Bolsheviks in Izmailovo when I noticed, sitting next to one of the patients in a small ward of four beds, a man whose face seemed familiar. It was Georgy Malenkov, the former Prime Minister who had for many years been Stalin's favourite and likely heir. He was visiting his wife, Valeria Alekseyevna, to whom he owed the start of his terrible career. Although he had aged and was much thinner, he was far from being decrepit, and he obviously took good care of his appearance and health. It was odd to be sitting a few steps from the man who had cold-bloodedly sent to their deaths and torment tens of thousands of just such Bolsheviks as this enormous hospital in Izmailovo had been built to take care of. It was even stranger to think that in other circumstances this man from another age could still have been sitting in the Politburo or running the government. He is after all only a few months older than M. A. Suslov, who died in 1982, and he is several years younger than A. N. Pelshe, who is still in charge of the Party Control Commission.

It is difficult to write even a minimal sketch of Malenkov, for he is a man without a biography. His was a life of special departments and privy councils. He had no image of his own, nor even his own style. He was an instrument of Stalin pure and simple, and his enormous power was nothing more than an extension of Stalin's own. When Stalin died Malenkov managed to hang on to the leadership of the country and the Party for little over a year. Stalin's legacy proved too heavy a burden for him, and he was unable to bear it on what turned out to be his rather feeble shoulders.

Georgy Maksimilianovich Malenkov was born in January 1902 into the family of an office worker. According to the brief official biography of him, when he was only 16 he went off to the front as a volunteer to defend Soviet power, and in April 1920 he joined the Party. He was a political worker at squadron, regiment and brigade level and was even employed in the political administration of the eastern front. According to the unofficial version of his biography, however, he was no more than a clerk in a political section and never roused the Red Army or the cavalry to the attack. He was a bad shot and could not sit a horse properly, but he was good at office work.

He did not return home to Orenburg when the civil war ended but went instead to Moscow, where in 1921 he enrolled in a technical high school. He soon married Valeria Golubtsov, who had a minor job in the Central Committee apparatus; this marriage was to prove the first step in Malenkov's remarkable Party career.

Until the beginning of 1925 he remained a student at the technical high school. Many student Party members in 1923–24 were attracted by Trotsky, and his supporters frequently had a majority in the student cells of the time. Malenkov, however, invariably toed the orthodox line and denounced the Trotskyist position. After Trotsky's defeat a commission was set up in Moscow to vet student Party members who had supported the opposition, and Malenkov, at the age of 22, was appointed a member. His work was closely observed. Urged on by his wife, he left the technical school just before completing the course and began working as a technical secretary in the Orgburo (Organizational Bureau) of the Party Central Committee. There he showed himself to be an excellent civil servant, and again his work was noticed. A couple of years later he moved up to become a technical secretary in the Politburo.

On the occasion of Malenkov's fiftieth birthday the Central Committee's official greetings spoke of him as 'a pupil of Lenin' and 'comrade-in-arms of Stalin'. Never once having met Lenin – he may just have seen him from a distance – Malenkov was, of course, no 'pupil of Lenin' but, like any other technical worker in the Politburo machine, he had met Stalin frequently at the small establishment in which he was subordinate to Stalin's personal secretary, A. N. Poskrebyshev. He did not remain for very long in this specialized work, however.

At the end of the 1920s Stalin managed to remove N. A. Uglanov from his post as first secretary of the Moscow Party committee, together with the entire organizational bureau of the capital, on the grounds of their being members of the so-called 'right deviation'. For a short time the new head of the Moscow organization was Molotov, and then in 1930 the Moscow Bolsheviks were given a new leader in the person of L. M. Kaganovich, and he it was who pushed Malenkov into more responsible jobs. He was put in charge of the organizational bureau of the Moscow Party committee, which was in practice the cadre, or personnel section, handling all appointments to posts on the Moscow district committees as well as the confirmation of secretaries in positions in all the most important primary Party organizations.

During this time Malenkov got to know a host of Party leaders and also young workers who had been given administrative jobs, such as N. S. Khrushchev. In Kaganovich's view, and indeed in Stalin's too, Malenkov carried out the purge of all former 'oppositionists' in the Moscow party organization most competently. In those days to be purged entailed as a rule only expulsion from the Party or demotion to a lower post, and arrests occurred only in extreme cases. After the Seventeenth Party Congress of 1934, however, Stalin set about restructuring the entire Central Committee apparatus in readiness for the more severe purges to come. He needed new men. He had known Malenkov for some time, and, since Kaganovich had the highest opinion of him, when the question came up of finding a new administrator for the top personnel section of the Central Committee Stalin's choice was Malenkov.

Almost simultaneously Stalin moved N. I. Yezhov into the highest positions in the Party hierarchy. As a Central Committee secretary, Yezhov took over from Kaganovich as chairman of the Party Control Commission, and a hostile rivalry sprang up between them as they vied to gain influence with Stalin, who of course did his best to fuel their animosity. Malenkov, who was not yet a member of the Central Committee, took

Yezhov's side and became one of his closest friends, while his relations with Kaganovich became unfriendly in the extreme.

With Malenkov's active help, Yezhov carried out a complete 'check on Party papers' in the first half of 1936. This was in practice another Party purge and the documentary preparation for the terror. A highly detailed personal file was compiled on each and every member of the Party.

Stalin was the chief organizer and instigator of the mass terror of 1936–38, but it was Yezhov who was the principal executor of the appalling and bloody campaign. He was appointed People's Commissar for Internal Affairs in the autumn of 1936 and headed the punitive organs that were invested with full powers to expose, isolate and destroy those whom it became customary to call 'enemies of the people'. In his very interesting book *Shipwreck of a Generation* Joseph Berger writes: 'unlike Molotov and Kaganovich, Malenkov bore no direct responsibility for the Stalinist terror of the 1930s.'[1] This view is mistaken. Malenkov operated in the wings, but he was decidedly one of those who, under Stalin's direction, activated the most important secret mechanisms of the terror. Formally, it is true, Malenkov was not working in any state organization. He was present as a delegate at the Seventeenth Party Congress but was made neither a member nor a candidate member of the Party Central Committee, nor was he appointed to either the Party or soviet control commissions nor even the central review commission. Thus he did not take part in Central Committee plenums, including that of February/March 1937 – formally speaking. Nevertheless, as head of the top personnel section of the Central Committee, he played just as important a part in the events of 1937–38 as did Yezhov, Beria, Kaganovich or Molotov. Invested with extraordinary powers, he exercised terror both in the quiet solitude of his office and on the spot in various republics and regions. In quite a few cases he was present when Party leaders were interrogated under torture. In 1937, for example, he went with Yezhov to Belorussia, where the Party organization of the republic was being subjected to little short of wholesale destruction. In the autumn of the same year he travelled with Mikoyan to Armenia, where again nearly

the entire Party and soviet establishment was devastated. A plan
of repressions that were to take place throughout all the regions
of the RSFSR was worked out with Malenkov's active participation, and it was in his department that new candidates
were selected for the jobs of regional and town Party secretaries
to replace those who had been arrested and shot.

In an attempt to disguise the scale of the terror, a Central
Committee Plenum was held in Moscow in January 1938,
ostensibly to discuss the question of 'mistakes [committed by]
Party organizations during the expulsion of Communists from
the Party'. Out of the seventy-one Central Committee members who had been elected at the Seventeenth Congress, only
twenty-eight were present at this plenum. Some had died;
nearly forty were under arrest. What is significant is that the
plenum discussed a report by Malenkov (who, as we have
noted, was not even a member of the Central Committee). The
January plenum did nothing to halt the terror, which continued
to rage throughout the country for many months to come.

Malenkov worked continuously and closely with Yezhov
throughout 1937–38. In the journal *Partiinoe stroitelstvo* (*Party
Structure*), which he edited for a while, one finds extravagant
praise of Yezhov, 'the Stalinist People's Commissar', 'the true
guardian of socialism'. He did not share Yezhov's fate,
however, and from the end of 1938 he began to co-operate just
as closely with Beria, who replaced Yezhov as head of the
NKVD.

Malenkov did not begin to emerge from the inner corridors of
power into the open political arena until 1939, when he headed
the mandate commission of the Eighteenth Party Congress and
reported on the composition of the Congress at its fifth session.
It was only then that he became a member of the Central
Committee; at the plenum of 22 March 1939 he was appointed
one of its secretaries and, along with A. A. Andreyev and
A. A. Zhdanov, joined the Secretariat under Stalin. From that
time he was a constant member of this Central Committee
organ, which under Stalin was, if anything, even more
important than the Politburo in the everyday political administration of the Party. He also became a member of the Orgburo

and remained in charge of the top personnel department, which was reorganized as the Central Committee Cadre Administration.

Gradually the areas with which he was concerned as a Central Committee secretary broadened. For instance, he was given the job of supervising the problems of industrial development and transport, and he gave a report on these at the Eighteenth Party Conference of February 1941, which was convened in order to review the results of the first phase of the third Five-Year Plan. After the Conference a Central Committee plenum elected him a candidate member of the Politburo, and thenceforth he occupied a firm place in Stalin's immediate entourage.

When the war broke out Malenkov became one of the first members of the State Defence Committee, much to the surprise of many observers, for he was not yet a full member of the Politburo. During the first months of the war he accompanied a number of special commissions to several dangerous sectors of the front, and gradually he began to specialize in various branches of military management, with the particular task of supplying aircraft to the Soviet Air Force. The enormous losses suffered by the Air Force in the first weeks of the war gave the Germans supremacy in the air until the end of 1942, but the balance of force began to change in 1943. Soviet industry was able to guarantee the Air Force a large number of more up-to-date planes, and by the time of the Kursk Salient defeats supremacy was shifting to the Soviet side. Some credit is due to Malenkov for his success in stimulating the production of aircraft, and for that achievement he was made a Hero of Socialist Labour in September 1943. At the same time he was put in charge of a committee of the Council of People's Commissars that was responsible for the economic reconstruction of areas liberated from enemy occupation.

In 1944, when Soviet victory was a certainty, the Central committee set up a special ideological meeting, under Malenkov's chairmanship, which took the decision to review and reassess the German classical heritage. A resolution was passed in particular on 'the shortcomings and errors of late eighteenth- and early nineteenth-century German philosophy in the light of history'. The meeting lasted several days. It was just at this time that Stalin expressed his idea – highly significant in form and quite absurd in content – that classical German idealistic philosophy was a conservative reaction to the French Revolution. He added that German philosophers were typically apologists for the Prussian monarchy and its disdain of the Slavonic peoples. It was decided to go ahead with the planned award of the Stalin Prize for the first two volumes of the three-volume *History of Philosophy* edited by G. F. Aleksandrov *et al.* (1940–3) but to withhold it from the third, as this was devoted to classical German philosophy.

In the autumn of the same year, 1944, Stalin called a meeting in the Kremlin that was attended by members of the Politburo and Central Committee Secretariat, republic and regional first Party secretaries and leaders of the defence industry, the Army and the state security organs. The topic under discussion was the 'Jewish question'. In his opening remarks Stalin expressed his support, though with certain reservations, for a 'more cautious' policy towards the appointment of Jews to leading positions in state and Party institutions. All those present understood perfectly well that he was talking about the gradual exclusion of Jews from important jobs. A more detailed speech was given on this occasion by G. M. Malenkov, who demonstrated the need for 'heightened alertness' in relation to the Jewish cadres. Soon after this meeting Party committees at various levels received a memorandum signed by Malenkov (later known in party circles as the 'Malenkov circular'), which listed those jobs that it was thought undesirable to give to Jews. At the same time, certain limitations were imposed on the admission of Jews to institutions of higher education.

Soon after the war Malenkov was placed in charge of a committee responsible for the dismantling of German industry. It was a difficult job, and he was subjected to criticism as a host of powerful agencies struggled to acquire as much equipment as they could. During this period a series of clashes took place between Malenkov and the chairman of Gosplan (the State Planning Commission), N. A. Voznesensky, and their relations deteriorated. A commission that was set up under Mikoyan to examine the source of their disagreements came out with an unexpected solution: to end the dismantling of German industry altogether and to organize instead the manufacture of goods for the Soviet Union in Germany as a form of war reparation. In spite of the objections of Kaganovich and Beria, this expedient was adopted by the Politburo.

The repressions of the 1930s had led to the extinction of hundreds of thousands of trained people and the advancement into high office of new appointees with little experience in managerial posts. However, although the war caused enormous loss of life and the depletion of material resources, it also brought about the advancement and selection of talented new army commanders, economic managers, state administrators, whose merits and achievements not even Stalin could ignore. One such group consisted of former Party and economic staff from Leningrad under the patronage of A. A. Zhdanov, whose own influence on Stalin in the sphere of the ideology and conduct of the Communist movement was plainly growing.

Malenkov became a full member of the Politburo after the war, as did Beria, with whom he had relations of complete trust, amounting almost to a political alliance. However, another new full member of the Politburo was N. A. Voznesensky, who was then playing a bigger role in economic management than Kaganovich, Mikoyan or Malenkov; and A. A. Kuznetsov, by now a secretary of the Central Committee, took over some of the functions that had hitherto been fulfilled by Malenkov. In the field of ideology and social sciences, where neither Beria nor Malenkov had ever felt particularly strong, A. A. Zhdanov and N. A. Voznesensky were plainly pre-eminent. Then in the second half of 1948 Stalin was frequently ill, and in 1949 he apparently suffered his first cerebral haemorrhage: the struggle for power among the members of his close circle was on.

For a brief time, even before Stalin's illness, Malenkov was a victim of this struggle. Using the poor showing of the Soviet aircraft industry as an excuse, certain of his colleagues staged a scandal involving Stalin's son, Vasily, that led to the arrest of

the head of the Air Force, Air Chief Marshal A. A. Novikov, of
Central Committee member A. I. Shakhurin, who had been
People's Commissar for Aircraft Production during the war,
and of a large number of aircraft industry personnel and Air
Force pilots. All these arrests reflected on Malenkov, who was
removed from his post in the Central Committee machine and
sent into exile in Tashkent, where, thanks to the considerable
efforts made by Beria to ensure his complete rehabilitation and
return to Moscow, he did not have to remain for very long.

Beria was conducting at that time a highly complicated
intrigue with the object of compromising A. A. Zhdanov,
N. A. Voznesensky and their entourage. Malenkov was willing
to help. His relations with Zhdanov had been extremely hostile
for a long time; in return, Zhdanov and his friends regarded
Malenkov as an illiterate upstart and in private conferred on
him the peasant-woman nickname 'Matryona' because of his
somewhat effeminate appearance. Beria and Malenkov managed to persuade Stalin, who was already irritated by
Zhdanov's and Voznesensky's theoretical pretensions, that the
Leningrad Party organization and the Leningrad upstarts harboured 'separatist' ambitions – and thus the 'Leningrad Affair'
took off. Its victims were the main figures in the Leningrad
organization under P. S. Popkov, the terror spreading first
downwards, embracing hundreds and thousands of Leningrad
Party and Komsomol workers, scientists and economic staff,
and then upwards, with the arrest of N. A. Voznesensky and
his brother A. A. Voznesensky, A. A. Kuznetsov, M. I.
Rodionov and several other senior personnel in the Party and
soviet machine.

Malenkov went to Leningrad in order to destroy the Party
organization, a task he had taken it upon himself to accomplish,
while Beria attended to the Moscow end of the operation.
Zhdanov, who had himself only recently masterminded a series
of ideological pogroms, was removed from the leadership and,
at the age of 53, died alone in his dacha, in circumstances that
have never been fully explained. After his death Malenkov
again became one of the top figures in the field of ideology, and
it was under his leadership that the anti-Semitic campaign
gathered force. When he heard that Stalin's daughter, Svetlana

Alliluyeva, had divorced her Jewish first husband, Malenkov insisted that his daughter, Volya, divorce her own Jewish husband, an economist and architect.

With Voznesensky, Kuznetsov and Zhdanov out of the way, Malenkov's influence in Party and state affairs increased significantly. As Molotov, Voroshilov, Kaganovich and Mikoyan found themselves manoeuvred further away from Stalin's immediate vicinity, so Malenkov was drawn closer and closer. When in December 1949 *Pravda* ran a series of long articles by Politburo members, dedicated to Stalin's seventieth birthday, Malenkov's was published first, followed by Molotov's. To those who understand such things, this was a clear sign of special trust. From 1950 to 1952 he was without doubt second in importance in the Party, a position that he owed in large measure to his friendship with Beria. At that time Stalin also introduced Khrushchev and Bulganin into his inner circle, but their power in Party and state affairs was still considerably less than Malenkov's.

Certain Western writers who have studied the history of Stalinism have greatly exaggerated Malenkov's importance. For example, in his book *The Technology of Power* A. Avtorkhanov writes: 'The present CPSU is the creation of two people, Stalin and Malenkov. If Stalin was its main constructor, Malenkov was its talented architect.'[2] This assessment is mistaken. It is wrong to call Malenkov the 'architect', still less the 'talented architect', of the Party structure. He was at most one of several 'clerks of works', and not the best of them by any means. It may have been precisely for this reason that he became one of the favourites of Stalin, who could not bear to have truly talented people around him.

As a member of the Politburo and secretary of the Central Committee, Malenkov not only controlled the Party machine in Stalin's name but also interfered in the development of industry and transport. But the main task with which he was entrusted was the management of agriculture, the realization of the 'Stalinist plan for the transformation of nature', which became the subject of a noisy propaganda campaign. He was quite unable to handle the vast schemes involved, perhaps because they were based on mistaken ideas of the real conditions of Soviet agriculture in the early 1950s.

As one of the leaders of the 'ideological front', Malenkov had the job of hiring and firing the editors of the main journals. When A. T. Tvardovsky was first appointed editor of the journal *Novy Mir* he had a conversation with Malenkov, who asked him what the difference was between a 'thick' journal and a 'thin' one. The question revealed unpardonable ignorance. Since the nineteenth century the term 'thick' had been used to distinguish serious literary journals from the less serious. A 'thick' journal was so described because of its content, not because of its size. But Tvardovsky did nothing to enlighten his superior: he merely remarked that 'thick' journals published novels in instalments. Malenkov, apparently, was content with the explanation. On another occasion a leading article in one journal printed in error the claim that the 'People's Democracies' were moving 'from socialism to capitalism' instead of 'from capitalism to socialism'. Malenkov, who had the job of dealing with this case of 'ideological sabotage', was 'lenient' on this occasion; the matter was handled without arrests and the miscreants got off with severe Party penalties.

Malenkov, Beria, Bulganin and Khrushchev were regular *habitués* at Stalin's suppers. By then Stalin's consumption of food and drink was often much less moderate than it had been formerly, and frequently Malenkov became so drunk that he would have to be carted off at dawn by the guards and left in the care of two or three servants, who would bring him round in his large bathroom. He would be incapable of resuming his work until the middle of the day. Nevertheless, he was in favour. At the beginning of 1952 the cinemas were showing the two-part feature film *The Battle for Stalingrad* – actors play the parts of the Soviet leaders – in which there is a scene portraying Malenkov's arrival at the front, apparently invested with full powers, and his discussion of Stalin with troops who have just come from the battle. As it was well known that Stalin had edited the film himself and had seen it a dozen times, Malenkov's appearance in it was regarded as a sign of Stalin's special trust in him.

No Party congress or conference had been held since 1939, which was a blatant contravention of the Party Statutes, and the need for such a meeting was becoming more and more insistent. It was not that the Party required to hear a report on everything that had happened since 1939; rather, it had become necessary to renew the Party leadership and to create a new Central Committee membership. An entire epoch had come and gone since the Eighteenth Party Congress. The war, post-war reconstruction, international policy and the new repressions had wrought a profound change in the character of the Party and state leadership. Some Central Committee members were under arrest or had been shot; some had died; others were no longer politically active. On the other hand, many of the new administrators who had emerged and were now heading large Ministries, agencies and Party organizations at a provincial or even a republican level were not members of the Central Committee.

In 1952 the job of preparing a new congress was entrusted to a special commission under Malenkov's chairmanship, and it was also to Malenkov that Stalin delegated the task of reading the Central Committee's report. This was a mark of great faith on Stalin's part; but the leader was in any case too old and feeble to read a three- or four-hour speech in front of a large audience (not that anyone outside his inner circle knew this, of course). This was not the main reason, however. The cult of Stalin's personality had reached such heights by this time that it would have been strange indeed to expect him to explain himself, as it were, in front of the Party and the people and to listen to any kind of criticism from the congress. Moreover, the post of chairman of the Council of Ministers, which Stalin occupied in addition to the General Secretaryship of the Central Committee, had acquired supreme importance, as it had when Lenin held it, and the role of the Party was altogether much reduced. (For example, the Party had no control over the punitive agencies, which answered directly to Stalin.) All this considered, Stalin did not see it as his responsibility to read the Central Committee's report at the forthcoming congress. Moreover, just before the congress was due to open the press carried a new article by Stalin entitled 'The economic problems of socialism in the USSR', which was at once proclaimed a 'classic' and a 'work of genius'. This *oeuvre* was to serve as the basis for discussion at the forthcoming congress, whereas the Central Committee's report was merely a formal requirement. Such was the position on the eve of the Nineteenth Congress.

According to Avtorkhanov, a behind-the-scenes struggle was going on between Stalin and Malenkov before the congress, in the course of which Malenkov 'dared to object openly to Stalin' and even scored a political victory over him:

> Even before Stalin's death, the Party and the Party machine were virtually in Malenkov's hands. . . . At the Nineteenth Party Congress in 1952 he gave the Central Committee's report, which Stalin really ought to have given himself. After that it was plain to everyone that either Stalin was placing confidence in him wholly and preparing a successor for himself, or Malenkov had become so powerful that even Stalin had to reckon with him. In view of what happened after Stalin's death, I regard the latter view to be the correct one.[3]

All this is pure fantasy. Malenkov would never have dared to answer Stalin back, let alone enter into any sort of argument with him. Only his complete obedience and unqualified loyalty could have provided the basis of trust on which Stalin founded his selection of Malenkov as *rapporteur* at the Nineteenth Congress. And this had nothing to do with Stalin's alleged search for an heir either. Far from being preoccupied by his death and its aftermath, Stalin had no thought other than to rule the country for a long time to come. He was even planning a new round of terror, and the Party congress was to serve as a preparatory stage in the campaign.

There is no need to dwell in any detail on the report that Malenkov read to the Nineteenth Congress — one could have mapped out its main features in advance. He did not speak about events that took place on the eve of the war, nor about the war itself, despite the fact that these were the main features of the period that had elapsed since the Eighteenth Congress. Instead he devoted the first section of his report to the weakened state of the world capitalist system as a result of the world war, to the deterioration of international relations, of which the Korean war then in progress was a manifestation, and to the cold war between the two world systems.

Considerable attention was devoted in his report to various aspects of the struggle for peace and to relations between the Soviet Union and countries friendly to her. Malenkov noted the success of Soviet industry, of which the gross output by the early 1950s had risen to twice the pre-war level. In wildly exaggerated terms he described the state of Soviet agriculture – producing, for example, greatly inflated figures for grain harvests that bore no relation to reality – and to the accompaniment of stormy applause he declared: 'the grain problem that used to be thought one of our worst and most serious problems has now been solved successfully, solved finally and irreversibly.'[4]

In less than two years it would be shown that the country was, in fact, suffering from an extremely acute grain shortage, that agriculture was experiencing a severe crisis and that the facts and figures about grain harvests produced by Malenkov in his report had been nothing but a tissue of falsification. The Soviet grain problem has not been solved even now.

In the section of his report dealing with the strengthening of the Soviet state and social structure, Malenkov echoed a well-known Stalinist theme – the need to fortify the state machine, including the punitive organs, by every available means. Speaking of the structure of the Party, he justified the mass repressions that had taken place before the war. According to him, the 1930s had seen the elimination of 'degenerates', 'capitulators' and 'vile traitors', who had stood poised in anticipation of a military invasion of the Soviet Union and had counted on being able, at that difficult moment, 'to stab us in the back, to the advantage of our people's enemies'. Malenkov went on:

> By destroying the Trotskyist–Bukharinist underground, which was the centre of gravity of all the anti-Soviet forces in the country, and by purging the Party and soviet organizations of all enemies of the people, in the nick of time the Party eliminated the possibility of the emergence of a fifth column in the Soviet Union and also prepared the country politically for its active defence.[5]

As was to be expected, in the section of his speech devoted to ideological problems Malenkov spoke above all about Stalin's recently published work, 'The economic problems of socialism in the USSR'. Turning to the problems of contemporary Soviet literature, he pointed to the absence of such genres as satire and declared:

> It is wrong to think that Soviet reality does not provide material for satire. We need our own Soviet Gogols and Shchedrins who, with the flame of their satire, can incinerate all that is negative in life, all that is rotten, numb, everything that puts a brake on progress.[6]

This was, of course, the most blatant demogoguery; all satire, even that written after the Nineteenth Congress, continued to be regarded as 'defamation' or 'slander'.

Malenkov also made an attempt to formulate a number of theoretical definitions. He devoted several minutes in his report, for example, to the 'Marxist–Leninist' definition of the concept of the 'typical', or 'typicalness'. According to Malenkov, 'typicalness corresponds to the essence of a given social-historical phenomenon and is not that which is merely the most widespread, frequently repeated or everyday.'[7] The scholar and literary critic V. V. Yermilov wrote in the preface to the first edition of his book on Gogol: 'Comrade Malenkov's pronouncements on the concept of the typical have the value of an original scientific discovery.'[8] Other scholars considering the same problem, however, discovered with some embarrassment that Malenkov's definition was almost word for word the same as that in an article on 'the Typical' in the first edition of the *Literary Encyclopedia,* printed over the pseudonym P. Mikhailov, which concealed the real identity of D. P. Svyatopolk-Mirsky, who had been arrested at the end of the 1930s and had perished in the camps.

The Congress appointed the new members of the Party Central Committee from a list of names that had been prepared by the Secretariat and approved by Stalin. What was unexpected, however, was the outcome of the first Central Committee plenum at which the leading organs of the Central

Committee were supposed to have been appointed. In opening
the plenum, Stalin proposed that the Committee appoint,
instead of the Politburo, the Presidium that had been stipulated
in the new Party Statutes. He himself then proceeded to read
out the names of twenty-five full and eleven candidate members of this new Presidium. The list included a number of
people who had never been part of Stalin's entourage and
some (for instance D. I. Chesnokov) whom Stalin had never
even met before. Stalin's proposal was approved, though it
provoked bewilderment among many members of the previous Politburo. Of this episode Khrushchev's wrote in his
memoirs:

> [Stalin] could not have compiled that list himself. Somebody
> had done it for him. I must admit I suspected that Malenkov had
> done it, that he had kept it quiet and not told us. I asked him
> about it later, casually, in a friendly way. I said, 'You know, I
> think you had a hand in it.' He replied, 'I assure you I had
> absolutely no part in it whatsoever. Stalin didn't bring me into it
> and he didn't give me any instructions so I didn't prepare any
> proposals.' Well, that only made us wonder all the more.[9]

A Presidium bureau of nine was also appointed, and after the
plenum Stalin created a further inner bureau of five men to run
the Party, consisting of himself, Malenkov, Beria, Khrushchev
and Bulganin. A Central Committee Secretariat of ten was
elected, in which Malenkov was expected to play the leading
role.

The question of Stalin's successor arose as soon as the top
leadership of the country learned of his illness and discovered
that his condition was hopeless. Cautious discussion about the
distribution of power took place at the bedside of the dying
leader. Malenkov talked to Beria about it, and Khrushchev
talked to Bulganin. Beria proposed that Malenkov should take
over as Chairman of the Council of Ministers, which was at
that time the most powerful post, and Khrushchev and
Bulganin agreed. At the same time, however, it was decided
that Malenkov should be relieved of his duties as Secretary of

the Central Committee and that a still smaller Secretariat should be formed, consisting of five men, S. D. Ignatiev, P. N. Pospelov, M. A. Suslov, N. S. Khrushchev and N. N. Shatalin. None of the five was recognized as 'First Secretary', but as Khrushchev was the only one of them who was also a member of the new, smaller Central Committee Presidium, he acted as chairman at meetings of the Secretariat. Nevertheless, it was Malenkov who, in the first months after Stalin's death, turned out to be the top man both in the state administration and in the Party machine. He acted as chairman at meetings of the Central Committee Presidium, and all decisions of a directive nature had first and foremost to be agreed with him.

He was also the first to speak at Stalin's funeral. His was a short speech, reminiscent in form of Stalin's well-known 'Oath', the speech that the former leader had made on 26 January 1924 at the Second All-Union Congress of Soviets, except that instead of Stalin's 'We vow to you, Comrade Lenin . . .', Malenkov said, 'Our sacred task is. . . .'

It goes without saying that Malenkov was faced immediately with a host of the most complicated problems, which he was unable, and did not wish, to try to deal with single-handedly. But nor was he willing to delegate to his deputies or the other members of the Central Committee Presidium any important political and organizational questions either. It was over precisely this matter that conflicts soon arose with Beria, who, on his own initiative, had made several important rearrangements in the MVD–MGB (Ministry of Internal Affairs and Ministry of State Security combined) and was carrying on as if he were assured in advance of Malenkov's approval of whatever he did. Malenkov considered himself a friend of Beria, but he had not the slightest intention of allowing himself to become a pawn in his hands. This led to a rift in their political friendship and to the secret agreement with Khrushchev that resulted in Beria's dismissal and arrest.

At the summer 1953 session of the Supreme Soviet Malenkov produced a number of important proposals to deal with economic problems. One of these was the significant reduction of taxation for the peasants and the cancellation of all previous debts for collective farms and their workers. He also claimed that from then on the Party would be able to devote more attention to the development of 'Group B' industries (that is, those producing consumer goods). In his view, the rate of production of capital goods could be slightly curtailed and the industrial capacity thus released used for the production of consumer goods that were needed by the population. These proposals earned him general popularity for quite a long time, especially among the peasants, for it was the first time for many years that the villages had enjoyed any relief. Among the simple folk, who of course knew nothing about his former activities, the rumour arose and stuck that Malenkov was a 'nephew' or even an 'adopted son' of Lenin. On the other hand, the intelligentsia viewed him with distrust, if not outright hostility. The poet Naum Korzhavin reflects these feelings in his poem 'About Russia':

> Surely all your destiny is not to be seen
> In the cold, dull gaze of Malenkov.

Nevertheless Malenkov worked hard. He held discussions with several leading economists, one of whom he asked to make any suggestions that he thought might improve the economic situation. At the same time, Malenkov was attempting to consolidate his position in the leadership, and with this in mind he proposed several changes. His relations with M. A. Suslov were very bad; they were worse still with Suslov's close friend, the First Secretary of the Lithuanian Communist Party Central Committee, A. Yu. Snechkus, whom Malenkov wanted to replace. A special commission was sent to Lithuania by the Central Committee, headed by an executive of the Central Committee machine, one Yuri Vladimirovich Andropov. The special commission did its work in Lithuania, but its members came to the conclusion that there was insufficient evidence to prove that the Lithuanian Party leadership had fulfilled its functions unsatisfactorily. The commission's report was approved at a meeting of the Politburo, which also approved a report by Snechkus himself, and he was allowed to remain in his post as head of the Lithuanian Party Central Committee. In these circumstances Malenkov decided that he could not proceed with his plan to get rid of Snechkus. After the meeting he went up to Andropov in a corridor of the Central Committee building and, taking him by the elbow, said to him in a low voice, 'I'll never forgive you for that.' In fact, Andropov was soon released from his post in the Central Committee administration and sent as Counsellor to Hungary. He was, however, promoted to Ambassador in 1954.

The removal of Beria led at once, if indirectly, to the weakening of Malenkov's power and influence. An important ally had disappeared from the leadership, and Molotov, Kaganovich, Voroshilov and Mikoyan had not the slightest sympathy for Malenkov. They were inclined to support the simpler and more straightforward Khrushchev. Many of the charges laid against Beria by the public prosecutor rubbed off on Malenkov, in particular the case of the 'Leningrad Affair'. Moreover, during the investigation Beria endeavoured to write various notes to Malenkov, who then had to try to justify himself to his colleagues in the Presidium (Politburo). The simple fact emerged that Malenkov, who had become accustomed to playing second fiddle under Stalin, was not a sufficiently strong character to assume the leading role in the Party with any confidence. He was afraid to take important decisions; he was hesitant and unsure of himself; he was unable to stand his ground when he encountered opposition. Work in the Party apparatus had not cultivated in Malenkov the qualities that ten years of independent work in the Ukraine had produced in Khrushchev. It transpired, moreover, that Malenkov did not really understand the problems and condition of the national economy, especially of the agrarian economy, which he did not even pretend to supervise. With relief he handed over the job of preparing all the basic reforms in agriculture, and the task of arranging a Central Committee plenum on agricultural problems, to N. S. Khrushchev, who was both in practice and formally the head of the Central Committee Secretariat, having become First Secretary of the Central Committee of the Communist Party of the Soviet Union.

The arrest and trial of Beria, culminating in his death sentence, were accompanied by a complete change of personnel in the punitive organs, at the head of which was now Khrushchev's close ally, General Serov. Simultaneously, the functions of the MVD–MGB were drastically curtailed. The punitive organs were no longer able to supervise the activity of the Party; on the contrary, they were placed under the firm control of the Party Central Committee, and in particular that of the Secretariat – that is to say, of Khrushchev. Unlike Stalin, Malenkov would be unable to use them as a base for his personal power.

By the autumn of 1953 Malenkov's role had been considerably diminished. The top Party apparatus was taking charge of all state and social organizations with growing assurance and firmness, and the first man in the Party now was no longer Malenkov but Khrushchev, without whose approval no important decisions or appointments could be made. By 1954 it seemed that only Khrushchev knew how to guide the cumbersome Soviet ship of state on its course, and it was he who initiated most of the important proposals for internal and foreign policy. Malenkov simply could not keep up with his energetic, busy rival; and, most important, he had no allies in the leadership who might have seen in him a boss and protector or who might have been obligated to him for their advancement and hence ready to do his bidding without reservation.

In these circumstances his removal from the post of head of Government was only a matter of time. When the rehabilitations began of all the victims of the 'Leningrad Affair' and, even more to the point, when it came to light that Malenkov was responsible for the appalling state of the country's agriculture, which had been concealed by his falsified data, he did not even attempt to struggle to retain his power or his leading position among the Party and state bosses. On 24 January 1955 an article by D. T. Shepilov appeared in *Pravda* entitled 'The general line of the Party and the vulgarizers of Marxism', which contained critical remarks that were plainly aimed at Malenkov, though his name was not mentioned. The next day a Central Committee plenum resolved to relieve him of his responsibilities as head of government. A statement was read out in which he acknowledged his mistakes and his responsibility for the parlous condition of agriculture in the Soviet Union, which he tried to excuse by reference to his 'lack of experience'. Several other members of the Central Committee and Presidium, including Molotov, came out with critical remarks against him, but they were not especially sharp. A few days later the minutes of the January plenum were read out to Party meetings throughout the country, and soon after that the plenum's decisions were formally approved by the Presidium of the Supreme Soviet, which also appointed Malenkov Minister of Power Stations. On the day of the plenum many of his relations and friends gathered at his mansion, which was one of a number that he had had built in the Mosfilm district, on his own initiative, for members of the Politburo. They were all nervous as they waited for their host to arrive. He came home very late and, on entering the drawing-room and seeing his family and friends there, said with obvious relief, 'Everything is as it was before!' They all understood him. No one had expected him to remain as head of government, but what he had told them meant he was still in the Central Committee Presidium, that he would be both a Minister and also a deputy chairman of the Council of Ministers. And that in turn meant that he would forfeit none of his existing privileges, that he would be able to go on living in this mansion and that his closest relatives would continue to enjoy their privileges too.

Having been replaced by N. A. Bulganin as chairman of the Council of Ministers, Malenkov seems to have maintained at least the appearance of good relations with Khrushchev. They visited each other's homes and attended each other's family celebrations. Perhaps Malenkov would have been content with this more modest role had he not been frightened by the policy of further debunking Stalin's cult of personality and of the deeper and more fundamental investigation of Stalin's crimes that Khrushchev was implementing. Malenkov spoke out against airing these questions at the Twentieth Party Congress in February 1956, but he was unable to stop Khrushchev from reading his famous speech. He himself spoke after Mikoyan but only uttered a few phrases about the harm of the 'cult of personality, which had belittled the role of the Party and its leading centre, had trampled on the creative energy of the party masses . . . and had led to peremptory personal decisions and arbitrariness'. Most of his speech was devoted to the problems of electrification.

The release and rehabilitation of millions of prisoners inevitably raised the question of Malenkov's responsibility, as well as that of the other members of Stalin's entourage, for the repression and destruction of innocent people, including not a few leading Party and state figures. To be sure, the Twentieth Congress did not go so far as to rehabilitate all the innocent victims of Stalin's purges. Even in 1957 Khrushchev had to insist on the rehabilitation of a large group of military leaders, including M. N. Tukhachevsky and I. E. Yakir, whose arrest and execution had been sanctioned in 1937 by the Politburo, of which Khrushchev was not a member at the time. An investigation was launched into the legality and grounds of the sentences passed at such fake political trials of the 1930s as those of G. Ye. Zinoviev and L. B. Kamenev, K. B. Radek and G. L. Pyatakov, N. I. Bukharin and A. I. Rykov, as a result of which dozens of the most prominent of Lenin's comrades-in-arms and leaders of the October Revolution and civil war had been condemned and shot.

For most of the members of the Central Committee Presidium Khrushchev had gone far enough; their patience was exhausted. United by their common fear of being blamed, Molotov and Kaganovich organized a factional group, which Malenkov joined at once. Its defeat spelled the end of his political and state career. Expelled from the Central Committee Presidium and the Central Committee, and removed from executive work in the Council of Ministers, he was given the job of manager of the Ust-Kamenogorsk Hydroelectric Power Station, which had been built on the upper reaches of the Irtysh and commissioned in 1954. Like Kaganovich, Malenkov was apparently an easy-going boss – so much so, indeed, that the Party obkom once admonished him for 'familiarity with the workers'. He lived in Ust-Kamenogorsk for over four years. Then in 1961, after the Twenty-Second Party Congress, he was expelled from the Party and sent into retirement. The Congress had heard a great deal about Malenkov's crimes, his intimacy with Beria and Yezhov and the fact that he had often been present during the interrogation and torture of prisoners. He had cause to feel that, once again, he had escaped lightly.

To leave the extremely exclusive and somewhat secret world of power and privilege and to enter the everyday world, with all its difficulties and problems, is hard enough for anybody who is removed from power, but it was especially difficult for a stand-offish man like Malenkov, who was unaccustomed to an ordinary way of life and who had found himself in the corridors of power of the Soviet Union since his youth. He would have found things more taxing still if it had not been for the support of his wife, Valeria Alekseyevna, who turned out to be tougher and more intelligent than her husband when it came to personal matters.

Malenkov has never shown himself to be sociable, and so it is not surprising that, twenty years after his expulsion from the Party, he should lead an extremely isolated life. Quite unlike Kaganovich, he practically never goes out in public or rubs shoulders with ordinary folk. He has never submitted his memoirs to journals; he is not to be seen at work in the reading-room of any Moscow library. It is quite likely that he has resolved not to record his reminiscences. (Not that he would have anything to say anyway, unless he were to tell the whole truth, as he knows it, about the Stalinist terror and his own friendship with Yezhov and Beria.)

He lives on the Frunze Embankment, in a pleasant apartment in the same house as Kaganovich, though they do not see each other, and Malenkov does not play dominoes. For much of the year he stays at his daughter's dacha near Kratovo, outside Moscow. Of his sons, both academic scientists, I have heard only good reports.

He used to ride around in an armour-plated limousine, but now, like everyone else, he has to buy tickets for the suburban electric train. He travels in silence, exchanging an occasional remark with his wife. He has become very thin, so that not even older people always recognize him, still less the young who have never seen his portrait.

Every summer he goes to rest and recuperate at Voronovo

Sanatorium, an institution reserved for official use by Gosplan. But even there he keeps himself to himself and rarely engages in conversation with the other inmates. His camera is usually slung over his shoulder when he goes out, and he spends his leisure time photographing nature. Once at Voronovo he ran into the old Bolshevik Yu. Fridman, who chanced to pick up a lens Malenkov had dropped. 'You know, Georgy Maksimilianovich,' Fridman told him, 'I spent fifteen years in the camps, thanks to you.' Malenkov replied that he had not known anything about this before. 'But I saw your signature on my file with my own eyes,' Fridman insisted. Not wishing to prolong the conversation, Malenkov quickly made off.

One hears rumours about Malenkov even now – for instance, that he has been baptized and attends church regularly. There are people who claim to have seen him in the little church in Mytishi or the one in the village of Ilyinskoye, near Kratovo. They also say he goes to the large Yelokhov church in Moscow, near the Bauman Metro station.

It was not the significance but the mediocrity of his personality that was concealed in the past behind his unsociability and distant manner. It would be wrong to suggest that he was a talented statesman whose capabilities were distorted or ruined by the terrible era of Stalinism. On the contrary, he was a man who was precisely fitted for his time, an era that sought out and promoted people like him. He is a squalid, evil man who has lived a squalid, evil, unworthy life. His crimes will not be forgotten, however devoutly he prays.

Epilogue

None of the subjects of this book can really be regarded as an outstanding political figure, for though all happened to play important parts on history's stage, none was either director or playwright of his own drama. Voroshilov was not a real military leader, though he commanded armies and fronts, even several fronts at a time. Despite his title of 'ideologist-in-chief' of the Party, Suslov was not a real theoretician or Marxist ideologist. Molotov was not a diplomat – a real diplomat, I mean – although for years he was the Foreign Minister of the Soviet Union. Kaganovich occupied one top post after another, yet he never learned to write a letter or note correctly. Malenkov was well practised in inner-Party intrigue but had little experience of genuine state administration. Mikoyan can be placed on a slightly higher plane than the others, for at least his intelligence gave him a better sense than they had of the boundaries beyond which he must not trespass if he wanted to stay alive.

Nevertheless, their lives are instructive and therefore of some interest to the historian, who should not select those whom he studies simply on grounds of sympathy or aversion. At the same time, this work was not prompted solely by the historian's intellectual curiosity, for there are certain lessons to be drawn from it, notably that when all is said and done, democratic mechanisms and institutions must be created in the Soviet Union that will ensure that people like Stalin and most of those around him can never again hold power or assume control of the country.

Notes and References

1 K. Ye. Voroshilov: Red Marshal

1 *Entsiklopedicheskii Slovar*, Granat, 7th edn, vol. 41, pt I, pp. 95–6, Moscow, 1926(?).
2 *Donetskaya Volna (Don Wave)*, no. 6, 3 February 1919.
3 *Leninsky Sbornik (Lenin Miscellany)*, vol. 37, Moscow, 1970, pp. 138–9.
4 For example, V. Yefimov and E. Gai, *S Nami Voroshilov (Voroshilov is With Us)*, Moscow–Leningrad, 1926; I. Vardin *Voroshilov Rabochy-vozhd Krasnoy Armii (Voroshilov – Worker-Leader of the Red Army)*, Moscow, 1926, etc.
5 *Stalin. Collected Essays for his 50th Birthday*, Moscow–Leningrad, 1929, p. 57.
6 K. Ye. Voroshilov, *Stalin i voennye sily SSSR (Stalin and the Armed Forces of the USSR)*, Moscow, 1951.
7 L. Nord, *Marshal Tukhachevsky*, Paris, Lef, 1978, p. 102.
8 *XXII-y s'ezd KPSS: Stenografichesky otchet (Stenographic Report of the 22nd Congress of the CPSU)*, Moscow, 1961, vol. 1, p. 105.
9 ibid., vol. 2, pp. 43–4.
10 ibid., p. 403.
11 ibid.
12 ibid., p. 553.
13 ibid., pp. 589–90.
14 K. Ye. Voroshilov, *Rasskazy o zhizni (Tales of Life)*, pt 1, Moscow, 1968, pp. 247–8.

2 A. I. Mikoyan: from Ilyich to Ilyich

1 *Rabochaya Moskva (Workers' Moscow)*, 18 November 1935.
2 *Kommunist*, Yerevan, 11 November and 8 December 1937.
3 *Pravda*, 20 December 1937.

4 Unpublished memoirs of Vladimir Gusarov.

5 Testimony of A. V. Snegov, the historian and old Bolshevik, who now lives as a pensioner in Moscow.

6 *Rabochaya Moskva,* 24 November 1936.

7 *Sotsialisticheskii Vestnik (Socialist Messenger),* New~York, 3 March 1951.

8 In the event the deportations took place after the Germans were driven out, but the news was not made known in the West until 1945 (Publisher's note).

9 N. S. Khrushchev, *Khrushchev Remembers: The Last Testament,* ed. Strobe Talbott, London, André Deutsch, 1974, p. 359–61.

10 *XX-y s'ezd KPSS: Stenografichesky otchet (Stenographic Report of the 20th Congress of the CPSU),* Moscow, 1956, vol. 1, pp. 301–27.

11 Quoted from *Russkaya Mysl (Russian Thought),* Paris, 5 February 1976, p. 7.

12 G. Svirsky, *Na lobnom meste (At the Place of Execution),* London, Overseas Publications Interchange, 1979, p. 136.

13 A. Ulam, *Stalin,* p. 392.

14 As a matter of fact, this is what happens to the archives of nearly everyone who has held an important post at any time.

3 M. A. Suslov: 'Ideologist-in-Chief'

1 A. I. Solzhenitsyn, *The Oak and the Calf,* trans, H. Willetts, London, Collins/Harvill, 1980, p. 302.

2 Mikhail Morozov, *Leonid Brezhnev: A Biography,* Stuttgart–Berlin–Cologne–Mainz, 1973, p. 91.

3 *XX-y s'ezd KPSS: Stenografichesky otchet (Stenographic Report of the 20th Congress of the CPSU),* Moscow, 1956, vol. 1, p. 284.

4 V. M. Molotov: Muscovite Pensioner

1 Hedrick Smith, *The Russians,* New York, Quadrangle/Times Books, 1976.

2 'Town-dweller' was a legally defined class in tsarist Russia, roughly equivalent in English to 'member of the urban lower middle class' (Publisher's note).

3 V. M. Molotov, *V. borbe za sotsializm (In the Struggle for Socialism),* Moscow, 1935, p. 76.

4 N. Y. Mandelstam, *Hope Against Hope,* trans. M. Hayward, New York, Harper & Row, 1970, p. 13.

5 N. Y. Mandelstam, *Vospominaniya (Memoirs)*, Paris, 1970, p. 167.

6 E. A. Gnedin, *Pamyat (Memory)*, Paris, no. 5, 1982, p. 391. The book to which he refers is A. U. Pope, *Maxim Litvinoff*, London, Secker & Warburg, 1943.

7 E. A. Gnedin, *Iz istorii otnoshenii mezhdu SSSR i fashistkoi Germaniei (Relations between the USSR and Fascist Germany)*, New York, Chalidze Press, 1977, pp. 34–5.

8 *Stenograficheskii otchet sessii*, Moscow, 1939, pp. 8–10.

9 E. A. Gnedin, *Katastrofa i vtoroe rozhdenie (Castrophe and Rebirth)*, Amsterdam, Alexander Herzen Foundation, 1977, p. 291.

10 William Stevenson, *A Man Called Intrepid*, New York, Harcourt Brace, 1976.

11 A. E. Levitin-Krasnov, *Ruk tvoikh zhar (The Heat of Thy Hands)*, Tel Aviv, 1979, pp. 105–8.

12 S. Mikunis, *Vremya i my (Time and Us)*, Tel Aviv, no. 48, 1979, pp. 161–2.

13 N. S. Khrushchev, *Vospominaniya: Izbrannye otryvki (Memoirs: Selected Extracts)*, New York, Chalidze Press, 1979, p. 96.

14 *Izvestiya*, 10 March 1953.

15 *Kommunist*, Moscow, no. 14, 1955, pp. 127–8.

16 Svetlana Allilyueva, *Tolko odin god (Just One Year)*, New York, Harper & Row, 1970, p. 353.

5 L. M. Kaganovich: Stalinist Commissar

1 Testimony of two delegates to the Bauman district conference, S. I. Berdichevskaya and M. Tsmikhles.

2 E. A. Gnedin, *Pamyat (Memory)*, Paris, no. 5, 1982, p. 365.

3 A. E. Kolman, *My ne dolzhny byli tak zhit (We Should Not Have Lived Like That)*, New York, Chalidze Press, 1982, p. 192.

4 Interview with A. V. Khrabovitsky.

5 Kolman, *My ne dolzhny byli tak zhit*, pp. 164–5.

6 *Ocherk istorii Ivanovskoy partiinoy organizatsii (History of the Ivanovo Party Organization)*, Ivanovo, 1967, p. 296.

7 *Literaturny Kritik (Literary Critic)*, no. 8, 1936, pp. 114–28. Other accounts suggest that Stalin's remark about Platonov was made after he had read *Doubting Makar*.

8 Joseph Berger, *Krushenie pokoleniya (Shipwreck of a Generation)*, Florence, Edizioni Aurora, 1973, p. 288.

9 A. Avtorkhanov, *Zagadka smerti Stalina (The Mystery of Stalin's Death)*, Frankfurt-am-Main, Possev-Verlag, 1976, p. 226.

6 G. M. Malenkov: the 'Heir' that Never Was

1 Joseph Berger, *Krushenie pokoleniya* (*Shipwreck of a Generation*), Florence, Edizioni Aurora, 1973, p. 294.
2 A. Avtorkhanov, *Tekhnologiya vlasti* (*The Technology of Power*), 2nd edn, Frankfurt-am-Main, Possev-Verlag, 1977, p. 634.
3 ibid., pp. 641–2.
4 *Pravda,* 6 October 1952.
5 ibid.
6 ibid.
7 ibid.
8 V. V. Yermilov, *N. V. Gogol,* Moscow, 1952.
9 N. S. Khrushchev, *Vospominaniya: Izbrannye otryvki* (*Memoirs: Selected Extracts*), New York, Chalidze Press, 1979, pp. 103–4.

Glossary

All-Union Communist Party (Bolsheviks)	the name of the Communist Party of the Soviet Union from 1925 to 1952
Central Committee	the body within the Communist Party that directs the activities of the Party between Party Congresses; each republic has its own Central Committee
Central Executive Committee	the supreme legislative body between 1917 and 1938; it was appointed by the Congress of Soviets
Central Rada	nationalist organization in the Ukraine in 1917–18, which formed the government of the Ukrainian People's Republic and concluded an agreement with the Austrian and German forces
Cheka	All-Russian Extraordinary Commission (for Fighting Counter-Revolution and Sabotage), the organization that was responsible for Soviet intelligence and secret police functions from 1917 to 1922. Thereafter the organization acquired other names: State Political Administration (GPU), 1922–23; Combined State Political Administration (OGPU), 1923–24; People's Commissariat for Internal Affairs (NKVD), 1934–46; Ministry for State Security (MGB), 1946–53; Committee for State Security (KGB), since 1953
collectivization	According to Marxist–Leninist theory, the voluntary co-operation of small rural producers

Comintern	the Communist International, an organization that unified the Communist Parties of various countries from 1919 to 1943
collective farm	*see* kolkhoz
Constituent Assembly	Russia's first fully representative Parliament, which was dispersed by the Central Executive Committee (q.v.) on 18 January 1918, the day of its opening, when it refused to recognize the Bolsheviks' first decrees
Council of People's Commissars	the name given to the first Soviet government, founded in 1917; subsequently the supreme organ of executive power, it was renamed the Council of Ministers in 1946
Dashnaks	members of the Armenian nationalist party Dashnaktsutyun, founded in 1890
GPU	*see sub* Cheka
KGB	*see sub* Cheka
kolkhoz	collective farm, an agricultural co-operative formed on the basis of common means of production and collective labour. According to Marxist theory, a kolkhoz is a voluntary union of free peasants
labour commune	a collective, organized on communist lines, in which all the means of production were owned collectively and profits from goods produced were shared equally among the members. Labour communes existed in the early years of the Soviet period, before collectivization and industrialization
Machine-Tractor Station	mechanical servicing and farm machinery depot on a collective farm (see kolkhoz)
Makhno movement	Anarchist movement in the southern Ukraine, 1918–21, led by N. M. Makhno. The Anarchists were ideologically opposed to all forms of government, be it Bolshevik or monarchist
Mensheviks	a tendency in Russian Social Democracy; until

the split in 1903 the Mensheviks and the Bolsheviks were known simply as Social Democrats and constituted a single party

MGB — *see sub* Cheka

Ministry of Internal Affairs — until 1946 NKVD (*see sub* Cheka)

New Economic Policy (NEP) — introduced by Lenin in 1921 in order to alleviate the heavy burden on the population that was imposed by the civil war (1918–21). It permitted private enterprise and was expected to last many years, but it was terminated at the end of the 1920s and replaced by collectivization and the Five Year Plans

NKVD — *see sub* Cheka

OGPU — *see sub* Cheka

Party Control Committee — one of the subordinate committees of the Central Committee (q.v.), of which the members are elected by Party Congresses. The body is responsible for ensuring that members observe state and Party discipline and reviews appeals against decisions to expel or otherwise penalize Party members

People's Commissar — the name by which the post of Minister was known between 1917 and 1946

People's Commissariat of Foreign Affairs — renamed Ministry of Foreign Affairs in 1946

Petlyura movement — Ukrainian nationalist movement, 1918–20, led by S. V. Petlyura (1879–1926)

Politburo — the political bureau of the Central Committee of the Communist Party of the Soviet Union – the Party's principal policy-making body, appointed by the Central Committee. Created in 1917, it has functioned regularly since 1919. It was known as the Presidium of the Central Committee from 1952 to 1966, when it reverted to its present name

Russian Bureau of the Central Committee	one of the two parts of the Bolshevik Party Central Committee that conducted revolutionary activity from 1903 until the Party became legal after the February Revolution of 1917
Russian Communist Party (Bolsheviks)	the name of the Communist Party of the Soviet Union from 1918 to 1925
Socialist Revolutionaries	from 1901 to 1923 one of the Russian revolutionary parties, of which the members were in many ways the heirs of the nineteenth-century party People's Will, which was peasant-orientated and endorsed the use of anti-government terror
soviet	literally 'council' – the basic governmental unit of the Soviet system
Sovnarkhoz	National Economic Council, provincial and regional body that directed industry and construction 1917–32 and 1957–65
Stakhanovites	participants in a widespead movement during the 1930s, 1940s and 1950s that was organized officially among workers who had to over-fulfil their work quotas. The movement began among coal miners in 1935 and was named after the miner A. G. Stakhanov (1906–71)
State Committee of Defence	supreme organ of military and civil authority during the Great Patriotic War, 1941–45
state farm	a state agricultural enterprise. Sovkhoz workers receive their wages in cash, whereas on a kolkhoz (q.v.) labour is rewarded partly with money and partly with agricultural produce
Supreme Soviet	the highest organ of government in the Soviet Union, nominally equivalent to Parliament
Workers' and Peasants' Inspectorate	an organ of state control that operated from 1920 to 1934

Select Biographies

Andreyev, A. A. (1895–1971) State and Party official. Politburo member 1932–52; chairman of the Party Control Commission 1939–52.

Antonov-Ovseyenko, V. A. (1883–1939) Leading Bolshevik. Commanded storming of Winter Palace in October 1917; held important military, political, legal and diplomatic posts after Revolution. Disappeared during purges.

Blyukher, V. K. (1890–1938) Soviet military leader, active in civil war. Marshal of the Soviet Union from 1935. Commanded Far Eastern Army. Shot.

Budyonny, S. M. (1883–1973) Soviet military leader. Commanded First Cavalry Army in civil war. Marshal of the Soviet Union from 1935.

Bukharin, N. I. (1888–1938) Leading Bolshevik. Active participant in October Revolution. Politburo member 1924–29. Chief theoretician of the Party after Lenin's death. Shot in 1938 after trial on false charges.

Bulganin, N. A. (1895–1975) State and Party official. Politburo member 1934–61. Minister of Defence 1953–55. Chairman of Council of Ministers 1955–58.

Dobrolyubov, N. A. (1836–61) Russian critic and political commentator of the mid-nineteenth century. Contributed to *Sovremennik* (*The Contemporary*), a leading journal of the period.

Frunze, M. V. (1885–1925) Leading participant in Revolution and civil war. Prominent military and state official. People's Commissar for Army and Navy Affairs 1924–25.

Grishin, V. V. (1914–) Party official and Politburo member since 1971. From 1967 first secretary of the Moscow city Party committee.

Kalinin, M. I. (1875–1946) Leading Bolshevik and state official. Member of Politburo from 1926. Chairman of Central Executive Committee and of Presidium of Supreme Soviet.

Kamenev, L. B. (1883–1936) Real name Rozenfeld. Member of revolutionary movement in Russia. Leading Bolshevik. Politburo member. Took part in inner-Party opposition movements 1925–27. Shot after trial on false charges.

Kirilenko, A. P. (1908–) Political leader. Politburo member 1962–82.

Kirov, S. M. (1886–1934) Real name Kostrikov. Leading Bolshevik and participated in the Revolution and the civil war. Politburo member from 1930. Head of Party organization in Leningrad. Assassinated by the terrorist Nikolayev in December 1934.

Kosior, S. V. (1889–1939) Party official. Head of Ukrainian Communist Party. Member of Politburo from 1930. Shot.

Kuusinen, O. V. (1881–1964) Took part in Russian and Finnish revolutionary movements. Later became Soviet state official and historian of Finland's revolutionary past. Member of Soviet Academy of Sciences.

Kuybyshev, V. V. (1888–1935) Took part in Revolution and civil war. Politburo member from 1927.

Lunarcharsky, A. V. (1875–1933) Soviet political writer, philosopher, literary critic, dramatist and Party official. People's Commissar of Education 1918–33. Died *en route* to Spain, where he had been posted as Soviet envoy.

Makhno, N. I. (1889–1934) Anarchist-Communist (see Glossary: Makhno movement).

Orzhonikidze, G. K. (1886–1937) (Sergo) Leading Bolshevik who took part in the Revolution and the civil war. Politburo member from 1930. Personal friend of Stalin. Committed suicide as a gesture of protest against the terror launched by the dictator.

Pelshe, A. Ya. (1889–) Party official. From 1966 Politburo member and Chairman of Party Control Commission.

Plekhanov, G. V. (1856–1918) Active in Russian and international social democratic movement. Founder member of the Russian Social Democratic Labour Party. Leading Menshevik after 1903. Eminent Marxist philosopher.

Poskrebyshev, A. N. (1891–1966) Head of Stalin's personal secretariat.

Saburov, M. Z. (1900–   ) Politburo member 1952–57.

Semichastny, V. E. (1924–   ) Chairman of KGB 1961–67, since when he has occupied lower-ranking posts.

Shelepin, A. N. (1918–   ) State and Party official. Politburo member 1963–76, since when he has held lower-ranking posts.

Sverdlov, Ya. M. (1885–1919) Leading Bolshevik in October Revolution. State official. Chairman of All-Russian Central Executive Committee 1917–19.

Voznesensky, A. A. (1898–1950) Brother of N. A. Voznesensky (q.v.) and, like him, an economist. Founded the Economics Faculty at Leningrad University. Rector of both Leningrad and Saratov universities. Minister of Education, RSFSR. Deputy of Supreme Soviet of the USSR. With his brother, caught up in 'Leningrad Affair' of 1949. Executed.

Voznesensky, N. A. (1903–50) Party and state official. Politburo member from 1947. Chairman of Gosplan from 1938. Economist and member of the Soviet Academy of Sciences. Shot.

Yagoda, G. G. (1891–1938) Head of NKVD 1934–36. Organizer of the mass terror campaign. Shot after trial on false charges.

Yakir, I. E. (1896–1937) Prominent Soviet military leader and army commander. Shot.

Yenukidze, A. S. (1877–1937) Leading Bolshevik. State official. Personal friend of Stalin. Secretary of the Central Executive Committee 1922–25. Fell into disgrace 1935; was removed from his posts and expelled from the Party.

Yezhov, N. I. (1895–1940) Head of the secret police 1936–38. One of the organizers of the mass terror campaign. Arrested 1939 and shot the next year.

Zhdanov, A. A. (1896–1948) Party official. Member of Politburo from 1939. Pursued extremely hard line with respect to ideology and culture.

Zinoviev, G. Ye. (1883–1936) Real name Radomyslsky. Leading Bolshevik. Friend of Lenin. Member of Politburo. Head of Petrograd Party organization. Took part in inner-Party opposition movements 1925–27. Shot after trial on false charges

Index